Women Journalists in Namibia's Liberation Struggle

Maria Mboono Nghidinwa

Introduction by Henning Melber

Women Journalists in Namibia's Liberation Struggle 1985–1990

Basler Afrika Bibliographien 2008

This publication is the result of a collaborative effort between its author Maria Mboono Nghidinwa, the Dag Hammarskjöld Foundation (DHF) and the Basler Afrika Bibliographien (BAB). The DHF recently initiated the Ernst Michanek Media and Development Event Series of which this publication is a first result.

©2008 The authors
©2008 The photographers
©2008 Basler Afrika Bibliographien

Basler Afrika Bibliographien
Namibia Resource Centre & Southern Africa Library
Klosterberg 23
PO Box 2037
CH-4051 Basel
Switzerland
www.baslerafrika.ch

All rights reserved

Basic Cover Design: Hot Designs, Windhoek, Namibia

The map on p.VIII has been adapted from "Contemporary Namibia.
The first landmarks of a post-Apartheid society", ed. by Ingold Diener & Olivier Graefe,
Windhoek (Gamsberg Macmillan Publishers), 2001.

ISBN Switzerland: 978-3-905758-07-8

Contents

"Struggles within the Struggle". An Introduction by Henning Melber   IX

Acknowledgements   1

1 Introduction   3
   Rationale for the study   6
   Goal for the study   8
   Research questions   8
   Researcher's personal motivation   9

2 Namibia's History and the Dynamics of Race and Gender   11
   Colonial history   11
   Early resistance   12
   Move to Independence   12
   Race relations   15
   Gender relations   16
   Namibian women in exile   17
   Overall role of women in the liberation struggle   19
   Status of women in independent Namibia   20

3 Namibia's Media History   23
   SWAPO media in exile   23
   Pre-colonial and colonial media in Africa   23
   History of the press in Namibia   25

4 Theoretical Frameworks   33
   Critical theory   33
   Ideology, hegemony and women   35
   Critical feminist media theory   37

5 Literature Review — 41
    Media in the struggle for liberation — 42
    Women in general in liberation struggles — 43
    Women in the media — 47
    Feminist media activism and gender and newsroom culture — 49

6 Methodology, Research and Participants — 55
    Qualitative research as an approach — 55
    The interview as a qualitative research method — 56
    Selection of participants — 57
    Procedures — 59
    Profile of participants — 60
    Data analysis — 60
    Reliability and validity of the qualitative study design — 60
    Secondary sources — 61
    Operational definitions of terms — 61

7 Women Journalists in the Struggle: Gender Constraints — 63
    Women had to work harder — 63
    Lack of promotions, hostile work environment — 65
    'Soft' news for women, 'hard' news for men — 65
    The glass ceiling — 68
    Gender consciousness in the newsrooms — 69
    Women journalists as mothers — 70

8 Women Journalists and Intimidation: Political Constraints — 73
    Government intimidation and death threats — 73
    Government 'black' list — 74

9 Black Women Journalists and Racial Constraints — 75
    The lack of support for black women journalists — 75
    'Sell outs' — 78

10 Resistance and Complicity — 81
Resistance — 81
Acceptance — 82

11 Reporting Injustices, Fighting Gender Inequality — 83
Reporting injustices and atrocities — 83
Fighting gender inequality — 86

12 Conclusion — 89
Theoretical implications — 90
Practical implications — 94
Recommendations for future research — 96
Limitations — 97

13 Appendix — 99
The participating journalists, their profiles, memories and assessments — 99

Acronyms — 135

Bibliography — 137

Index — 145

Namibia and southern Africa

"Struggles within the Struggle".
An Introduction by Henning Melber

One year into Independence, Namibia's capital hosted a pioneering UNESCO conference, which on the World Press Freedom Day (May 3rd) adopted the "Windhoek Declaration on Promoting a Free and Independent Pluralistic African Press" (1991). It was certainly no coincidence that Windhoek had been chosen as venue. Namibia's particular colonial situation as "a trust betrayed" and its singular status in terms of international law had been for decades of special concern to the United Nations Organisation. The country and its people achieved national sovereignty (declared on 21st March 1990) through a combination of a long and bitter anti-colonial resistance, including an armed struggle and militant internal mobilization against the South African occupation as well as UN based support by the overwhelming majority of the member states. The last steps to Independence were implemented with UN assistance and supervision, to obtain international legitimacy and recognition. Namibia joined the family of nations as a welcome member.

UNESCO's conference on the African media, held from April 29 to May 3, 1991, marked a milestone in the world body's new policy orientation, which recognized democratic movements in all societies as legitimate and the freedom of expression as an integral part of human rights. No longer were authoritarian governments able to justify media control and interference with reference to 'more important matters' and the protection of national sovereignty (cultivated as a handy argument to justify internal repression as 'in the people's best interest').

Already at the time of Independence, Namibia was blessed with a vibrant media landscape, in which even independent media were able to survive and to expose the violation of human rights under the Apartheid regime. The flagship of committed journalism, which was prepared even at high personal risks to name and shame whenever atrocities were committed, was the newspaper *The Namibian* and its courageous editor Gwen Lister. Not surprisingly, she also features very prominently (and rightly so) in this volume. Her initiatives in the mid-1980s paved the way for a human rights and democracy based media culture setting the standards to be measured against. As a journalist, she has since then remained a role model for any aspiring young professional seeking to define the bread-winning job also as an ethical challenge.

While at the forefront of democracy then, but castigated by the regime and its supporters as an agency of the liberation movement and therefore a 'terrorist subversion' acting on behalf of communist evils, *The Namibian* continued after Independence to maintain the tradition of critical journalism. Loyalty to the same ethical and moral values and norms, which required to take a stand against Apartheid and its inhuman practices, required to continue in the role as a watchdog against any form of abuse. By implication, the newspaper's task shifted from criticizing those in power then to criticizing those in power now, if they were violating democracy and human rights or showed other forms of disregard towards the electorate providing them the mandate to rule while claiming to act in the public interest. As a result, *The Namibian* rather sooner than later ended up once again as 'troublemaker' and its independent reporting was labeled as 'unpatriotic'. All of a sudden, it was accused of being a product of white supremacy and the arrogance of European foreigners – even though the stereotypes did not match with the empirical reality (meaning that almost all members of the staff are either black or Namibian and in many if not most cases both).

Against all odds, this newspaper has grown with the years and remains among the most influential print media in the country since over twenty years now. Its editor Gwen Lister continues setting examples of intellectual integrity guided beyond opportunism by a commitment to values and norms and not to individual power. The history of *The Namibian* is motivating for all those, who believe in the might of the pen (or computer, for that matter, given that the laptop has replaced both pen and type writer).

But even the example of *The Namibian* shows that one is hardly able to fight at all fronts. Racism and sexism are twin brothers (and mind you, brothers indeed, since they are mainly rooted in a concept of oppressive masculinity as reflected in male chauvinist attitudes and mindsets) which have or still are dominating societies. Under the given circumstances of South Africa's continued illegal presence in Namibia, the fight against institutionalized forms of racial discrimination by the colonial minority rule guided the commitments of the newspaper. It did not necessarily prioritize gender equality postulations and subsequent actions in favour of it.

Namibia, like so many of the Southern African countries, remains a male–dominated society also after Independence and its women face an uphill battle against entrenched forms of oppression. Horrendous cases of male violence occur on a daily basis and add to the sad conclusion, that ending a system of foreign occupation and racist minority rule is not the end of oppression and the beginning of liberation and emancipation in every respect.[1] While a sovereign state since 1990, Namibia is hardly a liberated society. Current

---

[1] See for example the recent chapters on various gender related aspects by Dianne Hubbard, Lucy Edwards and Suzanne LaFont in Henning Melber (ed.), *Transitions in Namibia. Which changes for whom?* Uppsala: The Nordic Africa Institute 2007.

trends among policy makers representing either the government or the former liberation movement SWAPO (now the political party equipped with a two-third majority in parliament and hence able to rule almost as it pleases) indicate a growing intolerance against critical reporting by the media and at times a personalized vendetta against individual journalists considered to be especially "difficult". *The Namibian* which once spearheaded the internal struggle in the public sphere with providing counter-information during the final years of South African rule, is now considered as hostile, if not the enemy's press: It operates under a boycott from the Namibian government, which places since the turn of the century not any longer any advertisements nor subscribes in state institutions to the paper (though everyone continues reading it). This illustrates the point that while power structures might have to some extent changed since Independence they continue to target the media. Those representing and executing the new political power use it like their predecessors to exclude, marginalize, ridicule and offend.[2]

While anti-democratic political attitudes have survived, sexist perceptions (and deeds) have so too. They go hand in hand with new structures of power. As we can witness, racism blends into a poisonous and at times lethal mix with homophobia, xenophobia and sexism. Seen in this light and in retrospective, it is also interesting to take note again of the documents illustrating the approaches during the years of the anti-Apartheid struggle. Maybe not too surprisingly, many of the views articulated then where rigorously anti-racist, but lacked any similar degree of anti-sexist convictions. Gender awareness was not a visible part of the commitment seeking to bring institutionalized forms of racist (or for that matter other forms of undemocratic) rule to an end.

As a matter of fact, even the Windhoek Declaration of 1991 lacks any reference to gender. The same must be said with regard to the recommendations and suggestions adopted by the participants in the "Seminar on Democracy and the Media in Southern Africa", organised by the Dag Hammarskjöld Foundation and the Foundation for Education with Production from December 1 to 5, 1989 at the Chobe Game Lodge in Botswana. It brought together a variety of (in total 26) independent media practitioners united in their fight against Apartheid and for democracy and human rights from all over the region. The seminar was among the first organized steps towards initiating and finally implementing the sub-regionally operating Media Institute of Southern Africa (MISA).

---

[2] Sadly enough, the personalized vendetta against Gwen Lister, which culminated on several occasions in outrageous insults and smear campaigns, is hardly any different in the polemical dimensions than it was during earlier days – although the risks for her physical integrity seem to have come to an end (an important fact, which is confirming that Namibia despite all shortcomings in its social and political system has made progress compared to the anything but so-called good old days).

With its regional headquarters based in Windhoek, it has become the flagship of independent media and media practitioners in the SADC region. It vehemently advocates and jealously guards over the freedom of the press against all odds in southern Africa. But even these activists seemingly failed then to discuss (or even to reflect upon) the gender aspect, as far as the published documents suggest.[3]

This volume is different. Earlier publications highlighted more generally the role of media in Namibia or even the role of media in the liberation struggle.[4] Maria Nghidinwa used the opportunity to turn her own professional experiences as a Namibian journalist into an empirical basis for a doctoral thesis on women as journalists in Namibia prior to Independence. She thereby is able to fill one of the many still existing gaps in our limited knowledge about social processes in the decolonization of the country. Such authentic historical records are an important point of departure to reflect further on and thereby address the ongoing discrepancies limiting the degree of true democracy in Namibian society.[5] Her study also reveals in concrete terms what is common knowledge in an abstract way: that there were always struggles within the struggle, at times of a different (but complementing) nature. The gender bias in the public sphere, not least the media and their reporting, is one of the cases in point.

---

[3] See the different contributions to the Foundation's journal *development dialogue* (1989:2) published under the thematic focus "'The Right to Inform and Be Informed' – Another Development and the Media". The publication is accessible for free download at the web site of the Foundation (www.dhf.uu.se). It includes a long article by David Lush on the initial years of *The Namibian*.

[4] See in particular the published work by William Heuva, *Media and Resistance Politics: The Alternative Press in Namibia, 1960-1990*. Basel: P. Schlettwein Publishing 2001, and "Voices in the Liberation Struggle. Discourse and Ideology in the SWAPO Exile Media," in: Henning Melber (ed.), *Re-examining liberation in Namibia. Political culture since Independence*. Uppsala: The Nordic Africa Institute 2003, pp. 25-33. Revealingly, Heuva illustrates in a sub-chapter on "Gender and the Struggle" (pp. 25-26) that the special efforts by women to voice their gender perspective was met with strong suspicions and reservations by the male comrades. The quarterly magazine "Namibian Woman" was launched by the SWAPO Women's Council at the end of 1984 in response to the lack of gender awareness among the men. Its focus on female emancipation as an integral part for the liberation struggle had a disturbing effect. According to one of the female activists of the time, who holds today high ranking government positions, "it was difficult to persuade men in the SWAPO leadership that their emancipation was not a 'type of European feminism' and that they were not fighting 'against nature'. (…) they were accused of luring women into 'lesbianism' and teaching them to hate men." (Ibid., p. 28) The at times vicious attacks and in-fights, which ultimately contributed to the collapse of any autonomous feminist activism affiliated to the liberation movement is well documented and analysed by Heike Becker, *Namibian Women's Movement 1980-92*. Frankfurt/Main: IKO 1995.

[5] A *Gender and Media Baseline Study* undertaken by MISA in Southern Africa during 2002 and published in 2003 showed that women journalists in all countries remain grossly under-represented. In Namibia, on average only every fifth news report in 2002 was a result of female journalists. Interesting enough, the state-owned daily newspaper *New Era* holds the least skewed gender balance. The summary of findings is accessible under publications at the MISA web site: http://www.misanamibia.org.na/.

I finally take the liberty to note with satisfaction, that the Dag Hammarskjöld Foundation was privileged to be actively involved in the finalisation of this study and its printed version. One of the Swedish participants at the seminar in Chobe mentioned earlier had been the late Ernst Michanek, in whose honour as former Director General of Sida the seminar was partly organized. He served for decades as a committed chairperson to the Foundation's board. Support to the autonomous media in societies of the South was always close to his heart, since he saw them as a relevant contributing factor to a democratic, human rights based society. That the missing gender aspect in the final recommendations of the "Seminar on Democracy and the Media in Southern Africa" is now almost two decades later presented in a different way, might have been the sign of respect he would have appreciated as a first visible result of the newly established Ernst Michanek Media and Development Event Series.

Uppsala, June 2008

Dedication

This book is dedicated to the future generations of Namibia, particularly to women; all my childhood friends; sisters, and brothers who have somehow managed to continue to strive in life despite rough beginnings in the SWAPO refugee camps – starting from the "Old Farm" to Nyango, in Zambia. Although my journey into academia, which began after the liberation struggle of Namibia, has not been easy due to the fragile educational system Namibians in refugee camps had to go through, I have somehow made it to this high point in formal education. True, it was challenging, but it was doable. Therefore, I would like to tell my peers that if I could make it, then they can also make it. I am a strong believer in the old adage: Where there's a will, there's a way! I would particularly like to dedicate this work to my mother, "meme" Susan Ndataneke Nghidinwa. God has truly blessed me with such a strong, loving, supporting and inspiring mother. You will forever be my hero, "Mee"! Last, but not the least I dedicate this work to my grandmother, Linea Kayone, my sisters and brother: Maila, Nangula, Takatu, Kirsti and Yesaya, and my nieces and nephews: Feiyo, Wendy, Emily, Lucy, Choco, Yesaya, James, and the twins: Ethan and Nathan.

Acknowledgements

First and foremost, my thanks go to the *Dag Hammarskjöld Foundation* (DHF) in Sweden – particularly to the Executive Director, Dr. Henning Melber – for its financial support during the last leg of the writing of my doctoral thesis. I am also grateful to the Government of Namibia that granted me a study loan during the initial years of my studies through its scholarship and training program at the Africa-America Institute (AAI) in New York. My publishers at the *Basler Afrika Bibliographien* (BAB), in Switzerland, particularly Petra Kerckhoff and Dag Henrichsen, have given me all the necessary support to see through the publication of this book.

Furthermore, my doctoral thesis, which culminated into this book, could not have come to fruition without the able support of my dissertation committee in the JHJ School of Communications at Howard University, Washington DC. Dr. Carolyn M. Byerly was not only my dissertation advisor, but my mentor as well. I often wonder how I could have survived the doctoral program without her unwavering support. I would also like to thank Dr. Richard L. Wright who also mentored me along during my years at Howard University. My thanks also go to Dr. Anju Chaudhary and to Dr. Clint C. Wilson, II for being part of my dissertation committee. I would like to express my gratitude to my External Examiner, Dr. Gretchen Bauer from the University of Delaware, who made very valuable contributions to my study at my oral defense.

My thanks also go to the head of my former department of Mass Communication & Media Studies at Howard University, Dr. Barbara B. Hines, (God Bless her soul!). Without her support, my journey towards achieving my degree would have been more difficult. Thank you to my professors: Dr. Gwang James Han, Dr. Abhik Roy, Dr. Robert Nwanko, Dr. Felicia R. Walker, Dr. Melbourne Cummings, and Dr. Anne Maydan Nicotera. I want to acknowledge as well Dr. Sulayman Nyang, from the Department of African Studies, Dr. Olayiwola Abegunrin, from the Department of Political Science, and Dr. Carolyn Stroman, from the Department of Communication and Culture at Howard University.

Special thanks also go to the current and former Namibian Embassy staff in Washington D.C, particularly former Ambassador Leonard Nangolo Iipumbu and his wife, meme Ndapewa, who gave me moral support to pursue this challenge to achieve a high degree in education which they believed would not only be my own personal achievement, but an achievement for the entire Namibian nation. I would also like to thank AllAfrica Global Media – Tami and Reed truly embraced me as part of the AllAfrica.com family! My thanks also go to all my interviewees for this study.

I would also like to acknowledge my classmates for their support during these four years at Howard University: Dr. Muhammad Hamisu Sani, Dr. Martin Yina, Dr. Kehbuma Langmia, Dr. R. Rashid Saad, Dr. Eric Durham, Dr. Gerald Folsom, Dr. Adrian Krishnasamy, Douglas Mpuga, Aquile Indigo, Franslee Thomany, Dr. Marnel N. Niles, Dr. Juliana Maria da Silva, Dr. Nickesia Gordon, Dr. Anestine LaFond, Dr. Annette Madlock, Dr. Kami Carey, Dr. Angie Copeland, Dr. Rachel Droogsma, Dr. Tia Mathews Tyree, Dr. Jocelyn Y. Johnson, Dr. Sherrie Wallington, Dr. Gladys Kamau, Dr. Shaunée Wallace, Gale Saunders, Candace Calloway, Dr. Gwendolyn Bethea, Patricia Karen Raper, and Dr. Terry Stephens, just to mention a few. I am also grateful towards my U.S.- based friends, family and colleagues: Sis Connie and Michael, Tega, Jussy and Karl, Kandi and Sasha, Rachel, Ester, Moonah, Ngadi, Diana, Auntie Elizabeth, Auntie Flora, Anyango, Mpho, Margaret, Tamko, Litta, Paulina, Mara, Grace, Anneline, Lucia, Dr. Yaw, Tjapaa, Dr. Kamatuka, Kondjai, Jephta, Baba, Babacar, Tamsir, Nyaka, Roger, Greg, Vincent, Mutheu, Evelyn, Aminata, Zik, Evans, Daafita, Pahukeni, Tate Kalomoh, Girma, Prata, Adao, Karl, Matias, Nii, Paul Francis, Josh, Gumisai, David and lastly, Luigi Cadet.

1 Introduction

The media have always played a pivotal role in national liberation struggles, and women have made significant contribution to many of these struggles. Women have often played important roles in affecting social change across the world while using different forms of media. British and American women abolitionists organized and printed pamphlets to raise awareness about the cruelty of slavery. American suffragists also used the media to campaign for universal suffrage, which was granted in 1920 through the enactment of the 19th Amendment to the Constitution. The American and British examples are well documented with historical records dating as far back as the mid-1800s. Women used the power of media, whether through radio, the printed press or newsletters to widely distribute the message. Unfortunately, it has not always been the same in developing countries, particularly in the region of Southern Africa where there has been a lack of scholarly attention to how women began to organize themselves in response to myriads of injustices against them. The study presented in this book was undertaken to address the critical imbalances that currently exist in scholarly studies of this region's modern history. Additionally, the study would make an invaluable contribution to those interested in the study of journalism history, international journalism, women and the media, and social movements and the media.

There is an extreme dearth of research on the role of women media professionals in liberation struggles in Southern Africa, particularly the nations of Namibia and South Africa[1]. Research in the area so far has led to one seminal work, William Heuva's (2001) *Media and Resistance Politics: The Alternative Press in Namibia, 1960–1990*. Regrettably, this work did not have, as a focal point, the role of women journalists in these struggles. For example, while Heuva's study of the role of the media in Namibia's liberation does a fine job of critically examining the evolution of the alternative press in Namibia, he did not quite go into details discussing the work of female journalists specifically, not even that of icons like Gwen Lister known for her courage in exposing the colonial regime's atrocities on the Namibian population. Furthermore, Heuva fails to adequately acknowledge the many other female journalists who played a long and extensive role in Namibia's liberation through their reporting.

---

[1] Throughout this book, references to South Africa are made due to the colonial ties between the two countries dating as far back as South Africa's 1920 League of Nations Mandate for the administration of Namibia to its illegal occupation of that territory in 1966 when the United Nation ended South Africa's mandate, which subsequently treated Namibia as its fifth province and extended its policy of apartheid to Namibia.

Meanwhile, in the second of a trilogy he began more than 20 years ago to investigate the role of the alternative media in the South African liberation struggle, Les Switzer (1997) sustained a critique of South Africa's white-dominated social order. In his first volume, he attempted to locate, identify and describe the hundreds of newspapers, newsletters, and magazines projected for the region's subaltern black (African, Colored, and Indian) communities. Switzer's (2000) third volume in this trilogy, *South Africa's Resistance Press: Alternative Voices in the Last Generations under Apartheid*, authoritatively captures liberation struggles in general, and provides a firm basis for understanding the South African transition from the apartheid era to black majority rule. To fill the gaps left by studies such as Switzer's and Heuva's, this researcher undertook a comprehensive study on the role and experiences of women journalists.

The need to document the courage and contributions of women who risked their lives to report injustices inflicted upon citizens who spent years under colonial rule in countries such as South Africa, Zimbabwe and Mozambique is a further reason why this study was a valuable undertaking. Indeed, the Washington, DC-based International Women's Media Foundation (IWMF), which makes annual courage awards, has honored female journalists from a number of nations with civil strife and/or oppressive regimes, including Namibia's Gwen Lister. Without such recognition, it might seem that these women don't even exist due to the dearth of documentation about them.

Lister, who in 1985 founded *The Namibian*, the nation's leading independent daily today, began her career at a liberal English-language newspaper, the *Windhoek Observer*. She left that position to start a publication that could freely and truthfully report the grave injustices and human rights violations under apartheid in Namibia. Needless to say, Lister, a leftist white Namibian, was constantly harassed, and at one point the South African military intelligence even sent a mercenary to assassinate her for criticizing the apartheid regime in South Africa (AWMC, 2004).

Unlike in Namibia, in South Africa there has been some scholarly attention – though minimal – to the important role of women journalists in the liberation of South Africa. Don Pinnock (1997) is one of a few individuals to examine the work of leftist journalist, Ruth First, publisher of the socialist daily, *The Guardian*. First, writing in the context of resistance politics during the 1950s, was one of the major activists in the struggle to eradicate apartheid in South Africa. In her writings, First documented the ways in which apartheid subjected both black indigenous South Africans and other people of color to atrocities.

There are at least three critical ways in which the role of women in social change in general, and liberation struggles in particular, has been under-estimated and under-investigated. First, at the broadest socio-political level, is the nature and extent of oppression at the intersection of race, class and gender within Namibian society. Second, at the level of the liberation struggle, are the specific ways that women faced gender-based oppression as advocates of freedom. Third, at the level of the work place, are the ways that women in varied occupational categories still had to fight for equality. The research presented in this book proceeds from the assumption that there is both scholarly and historical value in the accounts of women's journalistic experiences and professional contributions to African liberation struggles, which can be situated within the broader relations of gender, just described. It is against this background that this study was designed to examine the role of women journalists, black and white, in the struggle for Namibia's independence from South Africa between 1985 and 1990.

This timeframe, the researcher believes, was appropriate for the study since it begins when the media began to feature prominently in the liberation struggle. In fact, it was during this period that the country's leading newspaper, *The Namibian* was established by Gwen Lister, a woman journalist. This led to the period of subsequent media activism in the country that culminated in the nation's independence in 1990. *The Namibian* was founded by Lister as an alternative to the mainstream papers guarding the status quo. She was supported by many others, both of European and indigenous African descent.

However, it can be argued that technically the struggle for the liberation struggle of Namibia (the liberation war began in 1966) was coming to an end during this timeframe with the installation of the "transitional government of national unity" in 1985. This transitional government was constituted by six party members. The South African administrator-general was given the sole right of veto to any legislation. Additionally, the South African government was also in charge of the country's defense and foreign policy, without any indigenous mandate. As a consequence, the South West Africa People's Organization (SWAPO) refused to recognize it; it failed to gain legitimacy either domestically or internationally (Dobell, 1998).

It is important to point out that while the opposition press was becoming more aggressive during this period, further restrictions were also placed upon it by the transitional unity government. To begin with, the ability of reporters to cover the war was severely curtailed by the government, in that reporters were required to obtain a special permit from the police in order to visit the war zone in the northern part of Namibia (Herbstein & Evenson, 1989). Despite these restrictions, anti-apartheid newspapers, particularly *The Namibian,* didn't cower to the government's intimidation tactics. Indeed, it was due to this newspaper's success at the courts, where its lawyers ably argued against the R 40,000 'good behavior' deposit imposed on newspapers that gave rise to an increased radicalization of public opinion (Herbstein & Evenson, 1989). For example, the readership of *The Namibian* reached about 100,000, making it a necessary household name, and in fact, a paper that the army, police and government had to pay attention "to find out what Namibians were thinking" (Herbstein & Evenson, 1989, p. 167).

Rationale for the study

Scholars have long addressed the role of the media in fostering liberation struggles during revolutions and periods of internal crisis. While some have studied how the media have contributed to liberation struggles in Southern Africa, none of these studies have sufficiently examined the pivotal role played by women journalists in either South Africa or Namibia.

The study presented here proceeds from the basic assumption that Namibian women journalists played a pivotal role in the liberation of Namibia. For far too long, fields such as journalism have been male-dominated and inherently male-oriented in their perspective. According to Gallagher (2006), the third round of the Global Media Monitoring Project (GMMP), which is conducted among some six dozen nations every five years, revealed that news all over the world is still mainly reported and presented by men with the exception of television, where 57% of the presenters are women. Otherwise, women are in the minority in other media sectors such as newspapers, where only 29% of news items are reported by women journalists. The report further notes that female reporters are more likely to cover 'soft' news, while their male counterparts are more inclined to cover the 'hard' topics, which is news that is considered more 'serious'. The GMMP report further states that of all stories on politics and government affairs, only 32% are reported by female journalists worldwide, as compared to 40% of stories on social issues such as education or family relations (Gallagher, 2006). In the case of Namibia, the GMMP (2005) reports that 81% of television and radio presenters coded were women, while there were only, 15 (or 42%) women reporters coded in the Namibian media. When it comes to news subjects, only 25% were female (Gallagher, 2006, p.118).

Some female African journalists have long complained of not being taken seriously by their male counterparts, and of not being promoted to managerial positions. A delegation of Tanzanian women journalists to the 1993 Nieman Foundation, Africa-American Institute and International Women's Media Foundation conference held in Harare, Zimbabwe, raised their grievances of how male journalists treated them in Tanzania as "second class citizens". They reported that in Tanzania, for instance, women journalists face the problems of culture:

> That women are second class; we are supposed to be oppressed; we are supposed to be mothers; we are supposed to be in our roles [usually, women's role in a lot of African countries, if not all, is presumed to be in the kitchen]. We are not supposed to be in the male profession of journalism. So we get the problem of not being promoted because, supposedly, they have to ask your husband's permission (Nkamba, 1993, para.7).

According to these women, their male supervisors in the newsroom have also been reluctant to send them on out-of town assignments because these supervisors are required by cultural tradition to seek permission from these women's husbands. Another common excuse is that they could not afford to give assignments to female journalists who are mothers, in case their children became ill while they are away.

Women journalists' situation in the case of Namibia was even aggravated because they were not only operating in a male-dominated environment, but even worse; they were working in a war situation. One aspect of the present study explores whether some gender roles, defined by culture in Namibia, inhibited women journalists during the liberation struggle to execute their duties as reporters effectively. Historically, Namibian women, like other women worldwide, were subjected to gender roles that were believed to be complementary to their male counterparts. Hubbard and Solomon (1995) posited that although it is difficult to generalize gender relations in pre-colonial Namibia due to the fact that many of the country's many ethnic groups are matrilineal, while others are patrilineal, many communities had a sex-based division of labor whereby women played an equally important role as their male counterparts. They cited as an example that in the mixed-farming Ovambo communities, the harvest from the wife's plot was consumed by the household while the husband's was disposed by him for surplus profit (p.167).

However, these authors argue that despite the "complementary role" of women and men, ultimately the men still held the position of influence, with some exceptions, and that men usually had greater power for economic decision-making within extended family units. Hubbard and Solomon (1995) further state:

> While women's pre-colonial position was later interpreted as conferring inferior status, it has been asserted that notions of gender equality or inequality were simply nonexistent during this period and that men and women were perceived as inhabiting and controlling different and complementary spheres (p. 167).

Hubbard and Solomon (1995) further argued that the arrival of missionaries to Namibia began to undermine the traditional roles of submission and subordination as the norm for women. Echoing this latter sentiment in the context of liberation theology, Zedekia and Emma Mujoro (1989) posited that Namibian women were neglected by European Christianity, and were oppressed and forsaken by the racist policy of South Africa, "by the inherited and confused theologies of the African churches and by imitation and distorted Western culture" (p.105). These authors cited as an example that though women appeared in the forefront of mission activities during the Christianity era in Namibia, their role and status were considered secondary to that of men. They further stated that the Rhenish Mission did not consider any educational possibility for women in the church until a hundred years after its establishment in Namibia. Under the South African racist regime, Zedekia and Emma Mujoro claim that there was not a single area in which oppressed women, particularly black women, could experience emancipation, adding that they have suffered exploitation on the grounds of their sex, just like women elsewhere in the world.

Goal for the study

The purpose of this study is to examine the status and experience of women journalists during the liberation struggle in Namibia which could, in turn, have a bearing on the present and future status of women journalists in the country. It examines the gendered relations of power within then existing media structures in the country, as well as updates what has happened since independence in 1990. In so doing, this study documents and analyzes the specific contributions of female journalists to the liberation struggle in Namibia from 1985 to 1990. Analyzing first-person accounts of their experiences covering apartheid and the liberation movement, the study reveals how female journalists fared in the white-male dominated field. The study also assesses the constraints they faced. And, hopefully, this study sheds light on the invaluable contribution to the liberation struggle made by female journalists during Namibia's struggle for freedom.

Research questions

The study sought to build a baseline of information about the roles and experiences of women journalists in the liberation of Namibia. Using archival research and in-person interviews on location in Namibia, the researcher sought to answer these questions:

1. What gender and race-related constraints, if any, did Namibian women journalists confront in their news organizations during the liberation years?
2. How did women journalists deal with these constraints during that era?
3. What do they identify as their journalistic contributions to the liberation struggle of the country?

Researcher's personal motivation

As a female Namibian journalist who came to her occupation through her role as a freedom fighter in exile under colonialism, I have an interest in exploring my own and other women journalists' contributions and experiences in Namibia's independence. Having participated in the struggle of women in nurturing Namibia's liberation struggle, I now hope to turn a scholarly lens to the historical processes and personal experiences involved in that struggle.

Like many other Namibians, my family (parents and siblings) and I were forced to flee the country in 1974, after my father was repeatedly jailed and tortured by the South African police for his political activism as a member of SWAPO. Hence, I spent most of my formative years as a freedom fighter in a SWAPO refugee camp in Zambia. Just before my 17th birthday, I joined the SWAPO movement's military wing, the People's Liberation Army of Namibia (PLAN). What followed was a six-month training program at a SWAPO military training center in Lubango, Angola. The center trained thousands of SWAPO members in exile every year for preparation to take part in the battle that mainly took place at the border of Angola and Namibia against the South African Army. I trained as a political commissar[2] at the beginning of 1988 and remained in the training center as a political instructor (propagandist) until the implementation of the UN Resolution 435 that made it possible for exiled Namibians to return home in 1989.

While a propagandist in the training center, I also assisted in the women's office as a typist. Among many other duties, I was responsible for presenting the daily news bulletin that the high authority at the headquarters sifted from media organizations such as Voice of America (VOA), BBC, and Radio South Africa (RSA) to keep the trainee soldiers informed on issues concerning the struggle for the liberation of Namibia. This news was subsequently delivered by a team of political commissars, including myself, to our respective platoons at morning parades. Because of my work in the training center as a propagandist, I developed an interest in news reporting. A year after the independence of Namibia in 1990, I was one of four female reporters out of about 16 who were recruited to work as journalists for the Namibian Press Agency (NAMPA) in Windhoek, Namibia. NAMPA was founded in 1987 by SWAPO in exile. It was not a smooth ride for one to work as a female reporter in a male-dominated newsroom at that time. Not surprisingly, two other female reporters did not last at the news agency and only two of us remained for several more years before any others were recruited at the agency. As a reporter at NAMPA, I reported on developmental issues, including women's affairs, and at one point

---

[2] Political Commissar was a term used by the SWAPO party adopted from the Communist Party to mean an official assigned to teach party principles to a military unit.

I was assigned on the presidential beat (covering both local and international activities of the President of the Republic of Namibia). I also served as a committee member of the Journalist Association of Namibia and was a bona fide member of the Namibian Media Women's Association (NAMWA).

Meanwhile, although I was close to some of the women journalists I interviewed (some of whom I befriended during my younger days as a reporter in Namibia), I believe this "closeness" has not affected my objectivity in analyzing the data herein presented. In fact, I can argue that because of my background as a reporter, I was very comfortable with the journalistic discourse during the interviews, and since I am now an academic, I was able to incorporate my academic strengths with my past journalistic experience. Lastly, I feel that one cannot overstate the importance of women journalists and academics in this field in general and in this study in particular. If Namibia is an archetypal example of a larger international trend, namely the contribution of women in national movements, then one must appreciate and recognize the particular importance of women journalists and academics who strive to be a positive force for change. Indeed, women's involvement in liberation struggles in other parts of the world has been somewhat documented, as will be shown in the literature review undertaken in one of the following chapters.

2 Namibia's History and the Dynamics of Race and Gender

This chapter gives a brief overview of Namibian history and highlights how colonial and apartheid administrations oppressed the indigenous population. It also gives a brief overview of the emergence of the liberation movement. This serves as a backdrop against which Namibian women journalists used the media as a vehicle for social change.

Colonial history

Namibia's Declaration of Independence from the South African apartheid regime occurred on March 21, 1990, making it the last African colony to gain independence. The country then officially changed its name from South West Africa to the Republic of Namibia, although South West Africa had been known internationally as Namibia since 1968 when the United Nations General Assembly changed the territory's name (Dierks, 2002). Namibia's terrible colonial odyssey had begun more than 500 years earlier when a Portuguese sailor named Diego Cao set foot on that soil in 1486 and erected a limestone *padrao* (cross) at Cape Cross (Herbstein and Evenson, 1989; Dierks, 2002). A few years later, European powers increased their exploration of Namibia's coast. Widespread and organized Christian missionary activity did not commence until 1805. In 1878, Great Britain annexed part of Namibia, including Walvis Bay, which would later become Namibia's major port. In 1884, the entire country was annexed by Germany for "protection," making Namibia a full-fledged German protectorate. Indeed, the country was called German South West Africa in 1890, and its name was later changed to South West Africa when South Africa took dominion from the Germans. This latter name was kept for decades to come (Herbstein and Evenson, 1989).

During the First World War, South Africa was pressured by Britain to invade Namibia, and in 1914, German troops were pushed gradually northwards until their final defeat in 1915. This critical date marked the beginning of the country's colonial domination by South Africa. The country then became a League of Nations mandated territory under South Africa in 1921. After the Second World War, its status was changed from a mandated territory to that of a trust territory under the aegis of the United Nations. Like in South Africa, the indigenous Africans, known as the Bantu[1] became subject to territo-

---

[1] The name of the largest language group of sub-Saharan Africa.

rial demarcations[2] (Herbstein and Evenson, 1989; Cooper, 1991; Leys and Saul, 1995; Dierks, 2002).

Early resistance

As far back as the 1800s, indigenous Namibians resisted European domination. The labor strikes and protests by black Namibians in the 1890s to condemn low wages and poor working conditions in mines and farms (Sparks and Green, 1992) are typical examples of resistance to white domination in Namibia. Efforts to obtain legal recognition for unions were often shunned by the white administration, and it was not until the 1950s that a labor movement, barely accepted by the government, solidified in the country. The Ovamboland People's Organization (OPO) subsequently emerged as the largest of these early labor organizations and later evolved into the South West Africa People's Organization (SWAPO) (Sparks and Green, 1992).

By the late 1950s, many members of SWAPO began to flee South African apartheid brutalities in Namibia going into exile in Tanzania, Zambia, Angola and other countries in the region and abroad. In the 1960s, SWAPO was then consolidated in exile as a viable organization to campaign and champion the cause of South West Africa's liberation struggle. This was after U.N. General Assembly Resolution 1514 passed in 1960, which upheld self determination as a legal principle. This resolution strengthened SWAPO's position as a viable political entity (To Be Born A Nation, 1981; Dobell, 1998; Saunders, 2003). SWAPO designed a three-pronged strategy: the political front which entailed working with the Organization of African Unity (OAU), the Non-Aligned Movement, the United Nations, with Namibians back home; the diplomatic front, which meant working with individual countries such as the Nordic countries, the Namibia Support Committee, the Anti-Apartheid Movement in Britain, and in other countries in order to mobilize the international community to support Namibian independence . And finally, through the armed unit, the People's Liberation Army of Namibia (PLAN) which was launched in 1996 (Dobell, 1998).

Move to Independence

Beginning in the 1950s, internal and international pressure gained momentum and ultimately forced South Africa to release its hold on Namibia in 1990. Under the auspices of

---

[2] The apartheid regime used boundary demarcations such as 'homelands' and 'group areas' to maintain and enforce political control by white elite.

SWAPO the country started its armed struggle for independence from the South African apartheid[3] regime in 1966, the same year South Africa introduced the apartheid system in Namibia after the UN terminated South African mandate to rule "South West Africa" by the League of Nations. South Africa thereafter continued to occupy the country illegally until independence in 1990 (Cooper, 1991).

The term 'apartheid' was coined in the late 1930s by the South African Bureau for Racial Affairs (SABRA). The series of apartheid laws were enacted in 1948, and legislation supporting and enforcing the system was prominent between 1950s through the 1970s. Some of the initial 'apartheid legislation' included the Prohibition of Mixed Marriages Act of 1949, which prohibited marriages between white people and people of color; the Immorality Amendment Act of 1950, prohibiting adultery, attempted adultery or related immoral acts between white and black people; the Population Registration Act of 1950 which led to the creation of national register in which every person's race was recorded; the Group Areas Act of 1950 which forced physical separation between races by creating different residential areas for different races; and the Natives Act of 1952, commonly known as the Pass Laws, which forced black people to carry identification with them at all times (Herbstein and Evenson, 1989; Cooper, 1991; Leys & Saul, 1995; Eades, 1999). These laws were extended to Namibia during the white South African rule.

To this day, separate ethnic, linguistic and ethnic identity is prevalent in Namibian society mainly because of South Africa's previous policy of separate development (Herbstein and Evenson, 1989; Cooper, 1991). The policy not only meant the separate development of 'races', but also the separate development of ethnic groups, meaning that people were forced to live in designated areas called 'homelands' or reserves in rural Namibia. Furthermore, this policy ensured that there would be separate reserves for Basters, Caprivians, Damaras, Hereros, Kavangos, Namas and for the Ovambo ethnic groups. Similar division was extended to those who lived in urban areas, such that they were divided into separate locations according to their ethnic groups. And, of course, the white population occupied the more upscale areas of these urban areas (Suzman, 2002).

Similar to the German colonial era, which included the genocide committed against the Hereros and many Nama people in 1904, South African apartheid caused indiscriminate cruelty, human suffering, and oppression on a staggering scale by the military and police forces (Leys & Saul, 1995). It was very difficult for South Africa to release its hold on Namibia, primarily due to the latter's rich mineral resources, including diamonds. In

---

[3] Apartheid is an Afrikaans/Dutch word which essentially means segregation, and was a policy implemented by the National Party government of South Africa from the 1940s to 1990s to keep races (Blacks, Whites, Coloreds) in South Africa, and later in Namibia, strictly apart from one another in all facets of life.

1971, the International Court of Justice (ICJ) decreed that South Africa was illegally occupying Namibia and ordered it to withdraw immediately, but South Africa refused. In 1977, Western members of the UN Security Council formed the Western Contact Group, including Canada, France, West Germany, the United Kingdom, and the United States. The Contact Group then launched a joint diplomatic effort to bring an internationally acceptable transition to independence for Namibia. This led to Security Council Resolution 435 for settling the prolonged Namibian problem. U.N. Resolution 435 was adopted by the United Nations Security Council in 1978. In accordance with this resolution, the United Nations Transition Assistance Group (UNTAG) was deployed in April 1989 in Namibia as a UN peacekeeping force to monitor the peace process, and ensure free and fair elections. This process enabled thousands of exiled Namibians to return home to participate in the country's first free and fair elections in 1989. SWAPO was victorious in these elections, and in so doing they democratically ended more than 75 years of illegal occupation, a period during which thousands of Namibians died trying to end colonialism and apartheid. Namibia gained its independence on March 21, 1990 (Leys and Saul, 1995; Dierks, 2002; Gleijeses, 2002; Cooper, 1991).

Namibia's population today is relatively small, estimated at 1.8 million, with the country's geographical area at 828,268 sq, km. By comparison, neighboring South Africa has an estimated population of 44.7 million with a geographical area of 1,221,040 sq. km (Reporters Without Borders, 2004). According to the 2001 official census, 51.5 percent of Namibians are female, and about 33 percent of the population lives in urban areas. English is the official language, replacing Afrikaans in 1990. It can be argued that the latter now serves as a *lingua franca* in most parts of the country, particularly in the South. In addition, there are approximately nine indigenous languages as well as German. The country's average life expectancy at birth is estimated at 43.93 years, with males 44.46 years and females 42. 29 years (2006 est.). The literacy rate for persons aged 15 years and over is 84 percent (2003 est.) (World Factbook, 2007).

Geographically, Namibia is situated in southwestern Africa bordered in the west by the Atlantic Ocean, in the east by Botswana and Zimbabwe, in the north by Angola, and in the south by South Africa. It has, therefore, often been argued that the intensity of oppression and exploitation of the Namibian people under the South African apartheid regime worsened by the fact that the colonial power was territorially adjacent to its colony. Ya Toivo (1988) for instance, explained that while it took Britain weeks or even months to send expeditionary forces to its colonies to suppress anti-colonial opposition, it took South Africa only minutes to deploy its forces of colonial oppression in Namibia.

Race relations

During the apartheid regime in Namibia there was an extremely unequal social, economic and political relationship between the minority white and the majority black population which manifested itself in every aspect of society: housing, hospitals, employment and also the media. Every aspect of society was constructed on the basis of racial discrimination. What distinguished South Africa's apartheid era from segregation in other countries is the systematic way in which the National Party (NP)[4] legalized apartheid in 1948 in order to subjugate the black populations in South Africa and Namibia (Dierks, 2002). Hence, political and economic powers were seized and black Namibians lived under the yolk of apartheid where they were excluded from governing their own affairs. It is out of these circumstances that there was an emergence of resistance and self determination that culminated in the formation of a national liberation movement. Many of indigenous Namibians fled into exile and formed a resistance movement in the 1960s to fight through military and other means against the colonial regime (Dobell, 1998).

Further, black people had no economic power and participated only marginally in the country's economic activities, mainly as laborers in the mines, fishing and farming industries. There was a clear division of rank and status between blacks and whites in the formal industries. The economy was in the hands of the white minority who served their own interests. The indigenous pre-colonial system of communal property replaced in the colonial era with a system under which the means of production (land and labor) was owned by the apartheid regime (Herbstein and Evenson, 1989; Cooper, 1991; Leys and Saul, 1995). According to Hamutenya (1988), the indigenous people were forced to turn their labor power into commodity and sell it to the new, colonial owner of the means of production.

The Namibian black population's situation was well summed up by the then SWAPO's Permanent Observer at the United nations, Theo-Ben Gurirab. Gurirab (1988) pointed out that, in the centuries before colonial occupation, Namibia was inhabited by African people but in the process of colonization he posits that:

> Namibians lost their land; they lost ownership and control over the natural resources, which are their national heritage; they were reduced to mere labour units herded into fascistic labour reservoirs ('native reserves'), without freedom of choice, that is, the right to self-determination; in a word, they became slaves in the land of their birth; Namibians had ceased to be independent (Gurirab,1988 p.4*)*.

Gurirab (1988) further argued that the basis of the overall struggle of Namibia was to liberate the land, the labor power of the workers, the peasants and all the other victims

---

[4] The NP came into power in 1948 and was Nazi-influenced.

of colonialism and imperialism, and the natural resources and re-establish ownership and control over what was the Namibian people's national heritage.

Socially, black people were confined to segregated areas, segregated schools and Bantu education. They were restricted to marry within their own groups by apartheid laws such as the Prohibition of Mixed Marriages Act of 1949, which prohibited marriages between white people and other groups. Basically, blacks and whites were not even allowed to mingle and be friendly. White people who contravened the law also suffered the consequences as indicated in Chapter 4 by some of the women journalists interviewed for this present study.

Gender relations

Just like in race relations during the apartheid regime in Namibia, there were gender imbalances between women and men. Traditional Namibian societies were largely patriarchal and women's role centered around the home. There was polygamy, domestic abuse and a general lack of freedom to make decisions. Women were not included in leadership roles and their opinions were not deemed to be important in leadership. As the present study found, patriarchy continues to be the order of the day. Women's lack political and economic power, although it can be argued that since independence women organizations in Namibia have been quite progressive in pushing for women's empowerment (Hubbard and Solomon, 1995; Soiri, 1996).

In the context of the liberation struggle, it was a double-burden for black women: living in a patriarchal society, and also facing harassment and physical abuse from soldiers of the South African Defense Force (SADF) by virtue of their race. Women and children constituted the majority of those who remained in the villages while men were in the migrant labor system or left to join SWAPO abroad. According to Cleaver and Wallace (1990), because of their socio-cultural position, "women therefore bore the brunt of the systematic harassment and disruption of their lives, which characterized the military and police presence" (p.3). Cleaver and Wallace (1990) conducted extensive interviews with Namibian women to learn how they fared during those atrocious years. Many women spoke of their constant beatings at the hand of the SADF because they were suspected of partaking in "subversive" activities or breaking curfews, and harboring SWAPO PLAN fighters. The nightly curfew and restrictive laws made resistance more difficult and life even more stressful, these women explains.

Namibian women in exile

Although Namibian society was male dominated, the liberation struggle provided an avenue for women to participate equally alongside men in the movement for national liberation. The movement opened up opportunities in education, military engagement, and participation in decision making. The intensified struggle and increasing militarization of the northern parts of Namibia resulted in growing numbers of Namibians leaving the country in thousands in the beginning of the 1970s. There had been a constant flow of exiles into Botswana, Angola, and Zambia since SWAPO started operating outside of the Namibian borders. Most of the people leaving Namibia were from the Ovambo-speaking group. Initially, men constituted the majority of those who fled into exile; however, in later years men and women left in equal numbers. "Crossing the border became an option not only for men but for women as well. Students left in groups organized in schools, families fled together with their young children." (Soiri, 1996 p.74).

For example, in her article *We Left Our Shoes Behind,* Teckla Shikola (1998), an ex-SWAPO woman combatant, shares her own experience when she fled the country into exile:

> I left Namibia in 1977. I was sixteen years old. I fled with six girlfriends from secondary school in Oshaha, which is about 100 km from the Namibian Angolan border. The education system was bad and the conditions at our boarding school [in Namibia] were not good. Sometimes we used to have classes only once a week because South African soldiers disrupted the schedule. They would come to our school and beat us. Things were really very bad. (p. 139)

At the time, Namibians had one unified motivation to go into exile – to "fight the Boers" (Soiri, 1996). Therefore, it was common place for young boys and girls, even younger than sixteen years of age, to flee the country with their peers and in most cases without consent of their parents or guardians to go into exile with a mission to fight back the Boers. Shikola further recalls that:

> On our way [out of the country] we stopped at my father's place in Outapi, about 20 km from the border [of Namibia and Angola]. We spent the night there, but he didn't know where we were going. I left Namibia without my father's knowledge. If he had known, he would not have allowed me to go. People had been leaving the country since 1974 and nobody came back; you didn't hear anything about them, whether they were still alive or not, nothing. No, my father couldn't allow it. (p. 139)

Shikola said for her father not to be suspicious of their plot to escape from the country, she and her girlfriends decided they would each leave a pair of shoes at her father's place to give him an impression that they had just gone somewhere close by and they would come back soon.

Both men and women were eager to learn how to fight within the auspices of the People's Liberation Army of Namibia (PLAN), SWAPO's military wing. Because of this exodus of people, SWAPO had to establish refugee camps for the growing number of exiles in Zambia and Angola (Soiri, 1996). At this time SWAPO adopted an official policy of gender equality in the 1970s, which Soiri (1996) believes was later to be reflected in the Namibian constitution at independence.

In exile, women were accepted in the military alongside men and a SWAPO Women's Council (SWC) was organized during 1969–79 for the purpose of "mobilizing women to participate in the national struggle, [and to] make them conscious that they have the same right and obligation as men to make decisions concerning the nation's interests; that the woman should therefore develop herself to be a comrade in all aspects and not just a 'homemaker'; that both male and female should understand the system of exploitation and combat it as comrades" (Soiri, p.83).

SWC was started to advance the aim of national liberation. It focused on 'women issues' in refugee camps that included child care and political education. SWC representatives were sent to the organization's central committee as well as to international conferences. SWC recognized the fact that Namibian women were oppressed by their race and class, as well as gender. It believed that women were oppressed by the traditional structures and by the colonial system. However, only later was the concept of "triple oppression" applied: women were not only oppressed by their race and class but also by gender" (Soiri, 1996, p.84).

Despite the idea that women were fighting at an equal level alongside their male counterparts in the struggle, Soiri (1996) contends that gender inequalities were still experienced in exile. For example, the representation of women in SWAPO administration remained low during the liberation struggle, and by 1982 there were only three women in the Central Committee and none in the Executive Committee (Soiri, 1996). The SWAPO Women's Council in exile was also concerned that the position of women in Namibia was inferior (Soiri, 1996). Meanwhile, according to Cooper (1997), the SWAPO Women's Council has emerged to be the largest women's organization in independent Namibia.

Nevertheless, despite the traditional role of women in Namibian society, they played a significant role in all aspects of SWAPO's efforts including that of active combat. That women refused to be restricted to supportive functions, such as medics and couriers, but were fully trained and equipped as combatants, is clear evidence of a change in the perception of women's role within the movement (Cleaver & Wallace, 1990). This full integration of women was a result of consistent pressure by the SWAPO Women's Council to be fully and equally involved in the struggle at all levels.

Overall role of women in the liberation struggle

Namibian women participated in earlier struggles against the German conquest, and some, such as Anna "Kakurukaze" Mungunda are celebrated heroines who sacrificed their lives during the apartheid system in Namibia. On December 10, 1959 Mungunda led a group of Old Location residents in the Namibian capital Windhoek in a protest against the colonial South African apartheid regime for forceful removal from the Old Location to a place in the outskirts of Windhoek known as Katutura (meaning no place of our own) to make space for some white people who wanted this land. This protest left more than 10 people dead, and many others wounded. Mungunda was the only woman killed. Unlike the Old Location, the new location, Katutura, was such a long distance from the city and which meant a long and more expensive commute to the city (Henrichsen, 1997; First, 1963; Bauer, 2006).

However, despite the participation of women (such as Mungunda) in these historic struggles, Namibian women remained marginalized in the organization of their political liberation, and they only became visible as social and political actors with the movement of community organizations in the 1980s. South Africa's refusal to abide by the 1978 UN Security Council resolution 435 caused Namibians to intensify their struggle for freedom. During these years of a prolonged and bitter struggle for Namibia's freedom, major developments had taken place domestically. Furthermore, the more than 40,000 exiled Namibians began to re-organize in social movements such as the workers and students movements, and slowly these movements began to include many women activists. By the mid-1980s, Namibian women throughout the country had organized themselves around issues that affected their lives as women. At the same time, Namibian women in exile under the SWAPO leadership had organized themselves more firmly, and a growing awareness of movements concerns began to flourish among the exile community too (Becker, 1995).

After the country's independence in 1990, Namibian women had put themselves on the agenda with "women's issues" (Becker, 1995). These issues included domestic violence, alcohol and drug abuse, teenage pregnancy, the girl-child, poverty among rural women, and illiteracy. Iipinge and LeBeau (1997) also believe that Namibia's women's movements steadily gained momentum after independence. These scholars argue that Namibian women's participation, which included a 56-person delegation in the Fourth World Conference on Women in Beijing in 1995, was probably one of the most important events they embarked upon after independence. Those issues (mentioned above) topped the agenda of this female Namibian delegation to Beijing (Iipinge and LeBeau, 1997). Furthermore, although these scholars believe that the status and condition of Namibian women has markedly improved since independence in areas such as participation in decision-making in both public and private spheres, key leadership and policy-making positions are still male dominated (Iipinge and LeBeau, 1997).

Status of women in independent Namibia

The first few years following its independence in 1990, Namibia, under the SWAPO government, was considered one of the most democratic states in Africa with its Constitution guaranteeing fundamental human rights to all as well as freedom of the press. During this period, the Namibian media was, for example, found to be much freer than those of many other African countries. Indeed, according to the Reporters Without Borders' 2004 report, there were "no major obstacle to the circulation of news" in Namibia. However recent reports by the Media Institute of Southern Africa (MISA), documented in its annual publication: *So This Is Democracy?* indicate that over the past few years there has been an increase in media clashes with government including legal threats and censorship by government against the media (MISA, 2006).

Meanwhile, since Namibia's independence in 1990, several feminist scholars have examined the status of women in Namibia, with particular interest on female activism in the country. Scholars such as Becker (1995), and Hubbard and Solomon (1995), have found it difficult to claim that Namibia has one central and unified women's movement that speaks for all Namibian women. This diversity in the women's movement, they claim, is due to the country's historical racial and ethnic divisions that were caused by the pervasive South African policy of "divide and rule" prior to independence. These authors found that what exists in Namibia is not necessarily a formal and unified women's movement, but rather several distinct women's movements that, from time to time, rally together on issues of common understanding and belief. For example, Namibia has various nongovernmental organizations (NGOs) and governmental women bodies that, when necessary, join together to achieve common goals. Hubbard and Solomon (1995) argue that most formal women's groups in Namibia are spearheaded by black, urban, educated women, in a country where the majority of the population, including women, live in rural areas. However, because of the amount of networking and mutual support among various women groups in the country, these scholars argue that this warrants the use of the term "women's movement" in Namibia.

The women's movement includes bodies such as the Ministry of Gender Equality and Child Welfare, the Namibia National Women's Organization (NANAWO), Sister Namibia, SWAPO Women's Council, Namibian Women's Association (NWA), Women's

Action for Development (WAD), Differently Abled Women in Namibia and Namibian Media Women's Association (NAMWA) just to mention a few.

The Namibian Constitution is one of the few in the Southern African region, including South Africa and Lesotho, which is explicitly committed to eradicating all discrimination based on gender (Cooper, 1997). In fact, according to Cooper (1997), women are the only group of citizens in Namibia who were identified specifically to have undergone 'special discrimination' and hence, Article 23, Section 3 or the Namibian Constitution requires that a policy of affirmative action be pursued so that they can be 'encouraged and enabled to play a full, equal and effective role in the political, social, economic and cultural life of the nation' (Cooper, 1997, p.473). In fact, Namibian political analyst Joseph Diescho (cited in Cooper, 1997) has claimed that the Namibian Constitution is the first in the world to be written in gender neutral language. Namibian women were granted suffrage in 1989, enabling them to fully participate in their country's first fair elections that very year. At the time of independence, there were 13 laws that favored men over women, but many of these laws have since been changed or repealed. In their place, there is currently a body of law that is far more progressive and egalitarian, such as the Married Persons Equality Act (1996), Affirmative Action Act (1998), Combating of Rape Act (2000), Combating of Domestic Violence Act (2003), and Maintenance Act (2003) (Nandi-Ndaitwah, 2004).

The 2005 report of the International Institute for Democracy and Electoral Assistance (IDEA), produced in collaboration with the Electoral Institute of Southern Africa (EISA) and the Southern African Development Community (SADC) Parliamentary Forum, found that Namibia was among the top countries in the ranking of female parliamentarians. Namibia ranks seventeen in the world for women representatives in Parliament (Bauer, 2004). Indeed, by the time the Namibia's fourth National Assembly was inaugurated into office in 2005, 25% of its voting members were women – a phenomenon that indicates a steady increase in women's voting power. This is especially significant compared to the fact that, in the country's first National Assembly at independence in 1990, only 6 out of the 72 (8.3) voting members of Parliament (MPs) were women (Bauer, 2004; 2006). Similarly, the number of women at ministerial and deputy ministerial positions is also somewhat increasing in Namibia, in that, 5 out of 27 ministers in the country are women, while 4 out of its 20 deputy ministers are also females (Bauer, 2006).

3 Namibia's Media History

Significant to the proposed study is not so much the Namibian struggle fought through the barrel of the gun, but that waged through journalistic campaigns in the media. It might be said that SWAPO launched and maintained much of its liberation campaign through media. The war through the media was not only fought from inside the country but also from other media outlets within the frontline states, international media, and through SWAPO's own publications in exile.

SWAPO media in exile

For its own political agitation and mobilization, SWAPO produced several publications under the auspices of the Department of Information and Publicity, and other party wings such as the SWAPO Youth League (SYL), the armed wing (PLAN) and the SWAPO Women's Council (SWC). In 1984, the latter launched a quarterly, *Namibian Women,* through which women could air their concerns to the international community as well as among Namibian women in settlements (refugee camps) in exile and those in Namibia (Heuva, 2001).

In 1987, about three years before Namibia gained independence, SWAPO in exile launched the Namibian Press Agency (NAMPA) to cover the liberation struggle from its offices in countries such as Zimbabwe, Tanzania, Angola, Ethiopia, and in Europe and other places where it had offices. Other SWAPO publications were produced at its missions abroad on issues that sought solidarity for the Namibian cause. The anti-Apartheid movement, as well as the United Council for Namibia, also played a major role in producing specialized publications to support the Namibian people's struggle for justice. Other SWAPO publications were produced inside Namibia but they had to operate mostly clandestinely (Heuva, 2001).

Pre-colonial and colonial media in Africa

Like in many other pre-civilization societies, before the advent of modern mass media, mass communication in Africa as a whole took place in various traditional forms and by various means, among them talking drums, totem poles, artistic grave markings, sacred and secular art, itinerant bards, cultural societies, and palaver trees under which open discussions were held and disputes settled (Ibelema et al, 2004; Mwase, 1988). These forms of communication were, according to Schramm (1990) "… highly ingenious ways of storing knowledge and transmitting information", invented between the development of the present-day mass communication systems and the primitive times (p. 3). But the African way of mass communication was soon to be replaced by the European way. Successive colonial administrations managed to disrupt the cultural lives of a conquered people, causing a cultural obliteration through the introduction of new legal relations by the conquerors (Fanon, 1963).

In Africa, as a whole, there were three very distinct press traditions that emerged in the continent from the colonial era: the Anglo-American, the French, and the Portuguese presses. However, regardless of national tradition, the early presses in colonial Africa were generally organized to serve the needs and interests of the colonial administrations and European settlers. Rodney (1982) argues that the European colonialists established means of communication for their own benefit and not so Africans could stay in touch with friends and family, nor to facilitate trade in African commodities. He further explains:

> No roads connected different colonies and parts of the same colonies in a manner making sense regarding an African's needs and development – all roads led to the sea. Meant to extract gold, cotton, coffee, manganese: make business easy for the timber and trading companies and agricultural connection firms and white settlers (p. 205).

The Anglo-American tradition was the first European press tradition to be grafted onto traditional African communication systems. It was brought to the continent by freed slaves who were enslaved in places such as North America and the Great Britain and were allowed to return to Africa. With their knowledge from the new world, freed slaves started the first African newspaper in 1801 in Freetown, Sierra Leone. Denouncing slavery and slave trades were some of the beats carried on the first African newspaper, (Ibelema et al, 2004). They further claim that similar papers began to spread around the West African coast and to other parts of the continent, becoming the launching pad for political protests against the colonial administrations. This, for instance, forced the British colonial regime to promptly pass laws against such "sedition," and to censor offending newspapers in Ghana, Nigeria, and other African countries (Ibelema et al. 2004).

In the French colonial tradition, the development of the press in francophone Africa reflected the French policy of assimilation, a policy that aimed at transforming Africans in these colonies into "black French" people. According to Ibelema et al, in Portuguese colonies, although private Portuguese interest owned the press, it was part and parcel of the colonial administration machinery because it enjoyed government patronage and subsidies, and hence they were subject to arbitrary censorship.

History of the press in Namibia

In Namibia, the European version of mass communication began when Namibia's first colonial masters, the Germans, introduced infrastructure for their own convenience. They began with the establishment of railways in 1897, road networks and telegraphic communications in 1901 (Drechsler, 1966, Dierks, 2002).

The colony's first newspaper was published in Windhoek on October 12, 1898: the *Windhoeker Anzeiger* founded by Georg Wasserfall (Dierks, 2002). This was followed by numerous other papers which, historically, were divided into two: the German press for the interests of German settlers, and the Afrikaans press for Afrikaners. Black people were generally ignored by this exclusive media, until the founding of the first newspaper in Namibia published and owned by Africans, *South West News – Suidwes Nuus* (SWN) in Windhoek. Its first edition was printed on March 5, 1960. The only newspaper in the racially and ethnically segregated colony with non-racial and nationalist concept, SWN was published by the African Publishing Company (APC) in nine issues in English, Afrikaans, Otjiherero and Oshivambo. This Old Location[1] community paper was also supported by some liberal whites in the country at the time. It articulated the political and social ramifications of the colonial state and provided a platform for the incipient nationalist movement in Namibia. The paper went out of print with its last edition printed in September 3, 1960.

Meanwhile, to revive this historic paper, which is said to be largely forgotten in Namibia today, Dag Henrichsen of Basler Afrika Bibliographien compiled a facsimile reprint of the *South West News* in 1997 with all the issues ever produced. In his introduction to this facsimile reprint, Zedekia Ngavirue, the initiator and *de facto* editor of the *South West News* recalls that:

> In January 1959, the *South West Africa Progressive Association* (SWAPA) organized a reception to welcome me. It was held in the Sybil Bowker Hall of the Windhoek Old Location in conjunction with the Municipality of Windhoek who had newly engaged me as the first black Namibian social worker. In my address I stressed, *inter alia,* the importance of a newspaper for the black population of Namibia… this aroused an interest, not only among the educated Africans, mostly teachers, nurses, and clerks, but also among the few liberal whites (Ngavirue, 1997, p.8).

It turned out that Ngavirue was not alone with this thought. Others such as members of the African Improvement Society then serving on the Herero Chiefs' Council, Emil

---

[1] The Old Location was a place set aside in Windhoek by the apartheid regime for black people and existed well before 1905. In 1959 its residents were forced by the regime to move to another place on the outskirts of Windhoek known as Katutura (which means no place of our own).

Appolus and SWAPA had all been thinking of establishing a newspaper that would speak to the interest of the Africans and the Namibian society at large. After a few months of a feasibility study, Ngavirue and his colleagues established the African Publishing Company (APC). These budding reporters had to undergo an in-house training since only one of them, Appolus, had some experience in writing and laying out a newspaper. The rest went through elementary evening lessons on reporting and preparing a newspaper (Ngavirue, 1997). Ngavirue, along side Appolus, John Garvey Muundjua, Clement Kapuuo, and Uatja Willy Kaukuetu, David Meroro, was the founding director of the APC. He recalls that finding a firm that would not mind printing a black-run newspaper in Namibia was virtually impossible at the time. After knocking at several doors of printing houses in Windhoek with no success, they were forced to look further a field in the Union of South Africa (now the Republic of South Africa) where the black-owned Prometheus Printers and Publishers (Pty) Ltd., of East London agreed to print the *South West News*. Prometheus however just managed to print the first and second editions of the SWN as this printing house was raided during the State of Emergency in South Africa following the Sharpeville-Langa massacres in March 1960. APC was thereafter forced to look for another printing house back home, in Namibia. They finally found the Windhoek Printing Works and entered into agreement with them. According to Henrichsen (1997) the owner of the Windhoek Printing Works had just purchased new printing machines and was looking for business. By its ninth edition, the SWN could no longer be sustained financially and most of its editors had by then left for exile to fight for the liberation of the country from abroad. The SWN was therefore closed before publication of its tenth edition.

Towards the end of the colonial era, there were three distinct mainstream print media categories all falling under the broader category of the private/commercial press: 1) political partisan, 2)"independent", and 3) church press. Political partisan press included the *Allgemeine Zeitung*, which was founded in Windhoek in 1916 under the name of *Der Kriegsbote* (name was changed in 1919). The paper emerged from the war-time *Kriegsbote* in 1919, catering to German interests. It was published by John Meinert Printers (JMP). With the rise of Nazism in Namibia in the 1930s, it was absorbed by the *Deutscher Beobachter*, a version of the official organ of Hitler's National Socialist Democratic Party (NSDP) (Dierks, 2002). Another political partisan paper was The *Windhoek Advertiser;* the colony's first English-language newspaper was launched in 1911 as the official organ of the United Service Club, first as a weekly, then a bi-weekly and eventually a daily (Dierks, 2002). The final paper in this category is *Die Republikein,* which was born (in

1977) of the split within the National Party of South West Africa (NPSWA), founded as the official mouthpiece of the Republican Party. *Die Suidwester* was originally the mouthpiece of the NPSWA. It changed its name but remained the mouthpiece of the Aksiefront vir die Behoud van die Turnhalle-Beginsels (AKTUR), the other splinter of the NPSWA (Dierks, 2002).

Independent presses included the *Windhoek Observer*, which was founded in 1978 by Hannes Smith, a white Namibian journalist, with the goal of combating corruption, subversion and laziness through 'unbiased' reporting of social and economic issues. It fell prey to the South African apartheid rules for publishing political articles, and this resulted in its closure for two weeks in 1984 (Lush, 1989; Mwase, 1988). According to a report published in the New York Times on August 16, 1984, the authorities had accused the newspaper of supporting SWAPO which was waging a guerrilla war aimed at ending South African rule of Namibia (New York Times, 1984). SWAPO was deemed to be a terrorist and subversive organization by the West. This paper, which was deemed Namibia's only campaigning newspaper (for freedom and equality), soon fired its "controversial political writer", female journalist, Gwen Lister, when the paper became uncomfortable with her constant criticism of the colonial government, which caused the paper to be in conflict with the apartheid regime (Lush, 1989). Lush (1989) explains that when Lister left the *Windhoek Observer*, she took with her a group of like-minded colleagues who resigned in solidarity with her. Subsequently, the *Windhoek Observer* joined the ranks of those other media outlets in the country that were assisting the *status quo* (Lush, 1989).

Meanwhile, Lister emerged out of these turbulent years and exemplified the ever growing role of women journalists in liberation struggles, when she established her own independent newspaper, *The Namibian*. The founding of this paper was a watershed moment in the history of Namibia and indeed of the entire continent. According to Lush (1989), the decision to establish this publication marked the first time that a domestic publication published the truth about the events in the North where the majority of aggression and crackdowns were occurring to citizens. It was the first periodical that was widely distributed, and it gained popular support because of its commitment to human rights. This independent paper, which became the country's only 'alternative' newspaper, was in pursuit of free reporting. According to Lush (1989), the only alternatives were mass meetings that in most cases went unreported and were often violently broken up by the security forces, or by word of mouth. The paper's three broader objectives were to promote independence by publicizing the implementation of UN Resolution 435, to provide on-the-job training for aspirant Namibian journalists of all races, and to be the voice of the voiceless (Lister, 1995).

Namibia is a very low densely populated country with a vast landscape that has caused a lot of communication problems between regions in the country, hence before *The Namibian*, it was very difficult for the masses that lived out of the "war zone" (60% of the Namibian population lived in that war zone which was situated in the far north of the country), to know about the brutalities of the war (Lush, 1989; Mwase, 1988). In fact, the Namibian population's appreciation of the founding of such a media outlet is illustrated by some comments made by some Namibian women (and men) at the occasion of *The Namibian's* tenth anniversary which was published in the paper's tenth anniversary magazine in 1995. A Namibian woman activist Sima Luipert said:

> *The Namibian* played an important and significant role at a time when the Namibian and international public was deliberately misinformed on the political situation in Namibia during South African occupation … for the first time the eyes and ears of Namibians not resident in the war torn northern parts of the country were opened to the harsh realities of the war. The newspaper generally served as a source of information during a time when no alternatives were available" (*The Namibian*, 1995, p.7).

Another woman, Petrine I Shiimi, a Namibian businesswoman, added that "*The Namibian* has been the voice of the voiceless. Our cries have been heard throughout the world through *The Namibian*. *The Namibian* has always had the courage to speak the truth" (*The Namibian*, 1995, p.7).

Also congratulating Gwen Lister, on her newspaper's tenth anniversary, "as a woman and a leader" who "has always stood firm and been straightforward, aiming not to please people but to pinpoint the real problems," was Susan Nghidinwa, a former SWAPO Women Council Representative in Zambia during the liberation struggle. She further said about *The Namibian* that:

> This was the first newspaper to reach the Namibian people in exile. We started reading it right from 1985 in Lusaka (Zambia). By that time Namibia had become a closed country and *The Namibian's* dissemination of information about what was really happening was of great assistance to us in the struggle. The newspaper also gave prominence to the way Namibian women suffered under colonial rule and helped us to educate women to stand on their own feet. On coming back to Namibia in 1989, I realized that *The Namibian* was the only newspaper reporting the truth and giving constructive criticism" (*The Namibian*, 1995, p.7).

Other congratulatory statements were from former Secretary of SWAPO Women's Council, Pendukeni Ithana, who stated that: "When the history of the struggle for independence of this country (Namibia) will be written one day, *The Namibian* newspaper will go down as having stood firm in the fight for freedom and justice in this country. The newspaper used to be classified as 'the people's paper' (*The Namibian*, 1995, p.7). The then Vice Chancellor at the University of Namibia, Professor Peter H. Katjavivi said: "In the first years of its existence, the paper stood out as a beacon exposing the atrocities of the South African regime in Namibia" (*The Namibian*, 1995, p.8).

However, it can be argued that the ability of Gwen Lister's newspaper to report from the Northern part of the country rested with very few people who actually lived in that "war zone" area notably Oswald Shivute. Without reporters like Shivute it might have been more difficult for *The Namibian* to report from that region.

The third print media category was the Church Press. There existed numerous church publications in Namibia with the founding of *Omukwetu*[2] in 1901 and *Immanuel* in 1961. These publications were the mainstream ones and catered to information needs for a large number of the black communities. *Omukwetu* served the Ovambo people of northern Namibia, while *Immanuel* catered to south and central Namibia (Heuva, 2001). However, despite a highly controlled media environment, the anti-apartheid media were alive and effective in spreading the message of freedom and liberation. For example, the church press was quite nationalistic by carrying out very militant articles in support of the liberation struggle and in opposition to apartheid in the country. And like with other alternative press, the church staff were harassed by the colonial authorities. The printing works of the largest church, the Evangelical Lutheran Ovambo-Kavango church (ELOK) at Oniipa in northern Namibia, for example, was fire-bombed three times (the worst of these sabotage was in 1973). The Oniipa printing works published *Omukwetu* which carried political commentaries critical of the status quo (Mwase, 1988).

During the struggle, the country did not have a publication that focused specifically on women until the formation of *Sister Namibia,* launched in July 1989 just before the country's independence. This magazine was founded by a group of white and colored women activists who included journalists, artists, teachers, researchers, and community workers (Heuva, 2001). The magazine aims to highlight issues that affect women, be they political, economic, social, cultural or legal.

With regard to electronic media, the only broadcasting house in the count ry for both radio and television was the South West Africa Broadcasting Corporation (SWABC), a quasi-governmental institution which started as a relay station of the South African Broadcasting Corporation (SABC) in 1956. Just like its South African counterpart, SWABC catered to whites through Afrikaans and English languages, with occasional German inserts. When the liberation war was intensified, the South Africa launched an aggressive propaganda campaign in 1979, by instituting a language services, broadcasting in the main indigenous languages, giving birth to, for example, Radio Ovambo, and

---

[2] Omukwetu means *Friend.*

Radio Herero, among others in an attempt to win the 'minds and hearts' of the Namibian population (Mwase, 1988). During the war era, television was of no use to the indigenous people, particularly those in rural areas since their homes had no electricity. But radio soon became the main instrument to convey the apartheid regime's propaganda (Herbstein and Evenson, 1989). Keeping SABC linked to SWABC was a strategy to prevent the local population from listening to outside broadcasts because there were only FM/VHF transmitters, and the sale of AM receivers to the indigenous population was prohibited. Television, which was introduced in 1981, was also tightly restricted (Mwase, 1988). Programs were essentially foreign in content and outlook with no presentation in local languages. All programs were from SABC except those purchased abroad (Mwase, 1988). And also, the professional staff, engineers and operators in media institutions were either South African or German and were only hired secondly by SABC. The few Namibian staff were announcers and program organizers (Mwase, 1988).

During the South African colonial rule, foreign media were not permissible in the country, and there was virtually no community of foreign correspondents (Mwase, 1988).

The only foreign media permitted to function were state-sponsored South African newspapers, particularly the pro-apartheid publications. Anyone found in possession of foreign publications, especially those from communist countries, would face serious repercussions, including imprisonment (Mwase, 1989).

Today, the Namibian Broadcasting Corporation (NBC), which replaced SWABC has eight radio channels and one television channel which broadcast in six languages from the capital Windhoek, and three indigenous language transmitters in the north. BBC World Service, CNN and a range of South African and international TV channels are available via cable and satellite. Radio France Internationale is available on FM in the capital. There are seven commercial newspapers, of which three are daily, two appear twice a week, one is weekly, and one is a weekend tabloid (Namibia Trade Directory, 2004).

Meanwhile, Links (2006) contends that there were other publications in the country, such as *Bricks* and *Speak Out* which did not survive the early years of independence due to various, but especially financial, reasons.

> It also seems likely that these publications became redundant after independence, having served their purpose of fighting for a more just political, social and economic dispensation (Links, 2006 p.10).

Also Links (2006) notes that many of the activist journalists of the time also left these alternative media and moved on to positions within the new Government and other media, such as *New Era*, the NBC and the Namibia Press Agency (NAMPA) for greener pastures among other reasons.

Therefore, several mainstream publications, according to Links (2006) suffered the same fate as the community and alternative press and did not survive the early years of independence, hence quietly folding in the early years of independence (in the 1990s).

4 Theoretical Frameworks

Critical theory

The study presented in this book is broadly shaped by critical theory, a philosophical outlook concerned mainly with revealing, through scholarly investigation, the social stratifications and power relations. Unlike traditional theory, which seeks to understand and explain society, critical theory aims to change society by exposing the process of domination and oppression, which are often so deeply entrenched as to be invisible (Littlejohn, 2002; Morrow & Brown, 1994).

At its core, then, critical theory is a revision of the Marxist school of thought, which is concerned with liberation from all forms of oppression, and animated by a commitment to freedom, happiness, and a rational ordering of society (Bronner & Kellner, 1989). Ultimately, "the work of the critical theorists provides criticisms and alternatives of traditional, or mainstream, social theory, philosophy and science, together with a critique of a full range of ideologies from mass culture to religion" (Kellner, 1989 p.1).

Concerned as they are with liberation from oppression, critical theorists naturally align themselves with the interests of marginalized groups and view their task as uncovering oppressive forces through dialectical analyses aimed at shedding light on the underlying struggles between opposing forces. As argued by Littlejohn (2002), "only by becoming aware of the dialectic of opposing forces in a struggle for power can individuals be liberated and free to change the existing order. Otherwise, they will remain alienated from one another and co-opted into their own oppression" (p.210).

A natural outcome of the broad, emancipatory orientation of critical theory is that it is multidisciplinary in its scope, combining perspectives drawn from political economy, sociology, cultural theory, philosophy, anthropology, and history (Bronner & Kellner, 1989). Furthermore, "the theory consists of a number of loosely related theories challenging the dominant order of society including approaches such as world system theory, feminist theory, postcolonial theory, critical race theory, the theory of communicative action, structuration theory, and neo-Marxian theory (Littlejohn, 2002; McQuail, 1994).

However, despite the diversity inherent in these critical social science theories, they are bound by some common features, notably: (1) the belief that it is necessary to understand the lived experience of real people in context; (2) the examination of social conditions to uncover oppressive power arrangements; and (3) the conscious attempt to fuse theory and action (Littlejohn, 2002).

This scholarly tradition grew out of the Frankfurt School founded in Germany in 1923 at University of Frankfurt's Marxist School of Applied Social Research (Littlejohn, 2002; McQuail, 1994). Although the guiding principles for study and application there were furnished by orthodox Marxism, it was the first formally unaffiliated Marxist-oriented institute in Europe in that its members were never associated with any political party. Instead, according to Farrell and Aune (1979), "political interest soon centered upon objects for investigation: first with Marxist economics and the labor movement, and later with the less obvious patterns of domination in mass society, media, relational patterns, and even the ideologies of education and scholarly research" (p.95).

Max Horkheimer, a philosopher, sociologist and social psychologist, was one of the most influential directors of the institute, a position he assumed in 1930. His tenure would be characterized by a strong affiliation with scholars like Theodor Adorno, philosopher, sociologist, and musicologist; Friedrich Pollock, economist and specialist on problems of national planning; Herbert Marcuse, philosopher; and Leo Lowenthal, a student of popular culture and literature (McQuail, 1994; Farrell and Aune 1979; Littlejohn, 2002). Although there were a few others such as Walter Benjamin, who played an important role albeit not directly affiliated to the Institute, scholars such as Held (1980) have argued that any legitimate discussion of the 'Frankfurt school' must necessarily include these men. Among their significant undertaking was their effort to revise both the Marxian critique of capitalism and the theory of revolution in a bid to confront new social and political conditions that had since evolved following the death of its exponent, Karl Marx (Bronner & Kellner, 1989). "In the process, a critical theory of society emerged to deal with those aspects of social reality which Marx and his orthodox followers neglected or downplayed" (Bronner & Kellner, 1989, p.1).

In an ironic twist, members of the Frankfurt School were forced to migrate to the United States, after Hitler came to power in the 1930s, where much of their research was conducted from the 1940s to the 1960s (McQuail, 1994). Consequently, by the 1960s, many "so called" new left radicals in the United States and Europe turned for theoretical and political guidance to the works of the Frankfurt School scholars (Kellner, 1989). While in the United States, the Frankfurt scholars developed an intense interest in the role of mass communication and the media as structures of oppression in capitalistic societies (Littlejohn, 2002).

Currently, the best-known Frankfurt-influenced scholar is German philosopher Jürgen Habermas. His theory of universal pragmatics and the transformation of society has had considerable influence in Europe and an increasing influence in the United States (Littlejohn, 2002). In the late 1960s, Habermas, who represents the second wave of critical theorists, recast the notion of the theory in a way that freed it from a direct tie to Marxism or the prior work of the Frankfurt School (Littlejohn, 2002).

Today, scholars in mass communication, such as Switzer and Heuva, have used the critical tradition to examine issues such as the relationship between media ownership and content and the role of the media in social change including scholars such as mentioned earlier, have used it to examine the role of the alternative press during the liberation struggle of South Africa and Namibia.

Similarly, critical feminists scholars such as Byerly and Ross, 2006; North, 2004; De Bruin and Ross, 2004; and Joseph, 2004, just to mention a few, have also used the critical tradition to study women and the media focusing on issues such as newsroom cultures and the intervention of feminist in newsroom cultures. These scholars have also begun to use the tradition to problematise gender and media production by defining and looking at the gender sub-structures in media institutions (North, 2004).

Ideology, hegemony and women

Ideology and hegemony are some, if not the most important, concepts that are central to a better understanding of critical theory. The concept of ideology, which is important in most critical theories, "is a set of ideas that structure a group's reality, a system of representations or a code of meanings governing how individuals and groups see the world" (Littlejohn, 2002, p.211). Littlejohn (2002) further states that in classical Marxism, an ideology is "a false set of ideas perpetuated by the dominant political force" (p.211). Therefore, for the classical Marxist, science must be utilized to discover truth to overpower the "false consciousness" of ideology (Littlejohn, 2002. In fact, feminist media scholars, according to Byerly and Ross (2004), have understood that women have to move from that "false consciousness" to a place of consciousness about their circumstance and have begun to learn how to critique their experiences with the patriarchal society.

French Marxist Louis Althusser is a best-known theorist who believes that "ideology is present in the structure of society itself and arises from the actual practices undertaken by institutions with society" (Littlejohn, 2002, p.211). Littlejohn describes his position this way:

> For Althusser, this superstructure consists of *repressive state apparatuses,* such as the police and the military, and *ideological state apparatuses,* such as education, religion, and mass media … the repressive mechanisms enforce an ideology when it is threatened by deviant

action, and the ideological apparatuses reproduce it more subtly in everyday activities of communication by making an ideology seem normal. (p.211)

Before Althusser, nineteenth century theorist Karl Marx argued that an ideology operated more like a drug because it impairs the judgment of those who are under its influence and thus failing to see how they are being exploited. Further, people who are under the influence of an ideology are deceived to an extent that they undermine their own interests and behave in ways that increase the power of the dominant class on the expense of their own wellness (Baran & Davis,1995). It was on the basis of this premise that Marx concluded that, the only hope for social change was through a revolution in which the masses seized control of the means of production and control of the superstructure would naturally follow. This had to be done because the elites, he argued, would never willingly surrender power (Baran & Davis, 1995).

It was Althusser who devised the concept of *ideological state apparatuses* (ISAs) to refer to institutions such as religion, education, politics, the law, the family, media and culture, institutions believed to function as agents of the state and the ruling class although relatively autonomous from it. According to van Zoonen (1994), ISA's are "ideological battlegrounds that betray the contradictions within dominant ideology" (p.24). In the end, however, Althusser believed ISAs will function in favor of dominant ideology, an assumption van Zoonen (1994) criticized, arguing that Althusser failed to explain exactly why and how this is achieved.

Meanwhile, scholars have contended that Italian Marxist Antonio Gramsci's notes on 'hegemony' provide an important addition to the concept of ideology. Borrowed from Gramsci's term for a ruling ideology (van Zoonen, 1994; McQuail, 1994), hegemony is the notion that the ideas of the ruling class in society become those of the society in general (McQuail, 1994; van Zoonen, 1994; Littlejohn, 2002; Severn and Tankard, Jr.,1992). These scholars argue that the concept helps to converge varying ideas about how the culture of media (news, entertainment, fiction) assists in maintaining the class-divided and class-dominated society. McQuail (1994) further explains that:

> Hegemony refers to a loosely interrelated set of ruling ideas permeating a society, but in such a way as to make the established order of power and values appear natural, taken-for granted and common-sensical. A ruling ideology is not imposed but appears to exist by virtue of an unquestioned consensus (McQuail, 1994, p.99).

The mass media, for example, are perceived to be controlled by the dominant class in society and are known to be catalyst in exerting the control of that class over the society (van Zoonen,1994; Severin & Tankard, Jr.,(1992). For instance, in theories of ideology, media are viewed as hegemonic institutions that present the capitalist and patriarchal order as 'normal'. In other words, media represent one of the key agencies in civil society that make the construction of both hegemony and counter-hegemony possible. In the case of Namibia during the liberation struggle, for example, the alternative press provided one of the means for constructing a counter-hegemonic order – countering the apartheid domination of the Namibian masses (Heuva, 2001).

Similarly, in feminist terminology, according to van Zoonen (1994), media are thought to transmit sexist, patriarchal or capitalist values to contribute to the maintenance of a social order in which men maintain superiority. And, generally, feminist critiques argue that patriarchy (male domination) and capitalism are intertwined systems that perpetuate a male hegemonic system in media industries (Byerly, 2004). Therefore, critical feminist scholars have adapted Gramsci's concept of *hegemony* to assist in explaining the ways in which media aid in securing men's dominance in society (Ross & Byerly, 2004). Feminist scholars have been attracted to the hegemony concept because "it offers an analysis of how both men and women come to participate in a social system that is inherently unequal, and therefore undemocratic" (Ross & Byerly, 2004, p.3).

Critical feminist media theory

Critical feminist theory argues that how "media represent the female subject and the *experiences of women working in media organizations* are the product of a world system of patriarchal capitalism" (Byerly & Ross, 2006, p. 75 emphasis added).

Feminist media scholarship, which emerged in the 1970s, is concerned with relationships of power in both mass media and alternative media formats. The theory emerged in large part out of concern over the absence of women in news, the misrepresentation and misreporting of their experiences and their roles in society, as well as the many obstacles that prevent their advancement in media organizations. These issues were perceived to be associated with the general public's understanding about women's inequality, and the political discourse that was required for their advancement within their societies. This concern, in turn, invoked women's liberation movements around the globe to improve and increase the coverage of women's issues and social contributions, and to address issues of discrimination against women in media employment (van Zoonen, 1994; Gottfried, 1996). A few feminist scholars have so far examined media structures where men's ownership and domination is still the norm and where women have great difficulty gaining access to information regardless of their professional training, Byerly and Ross (2006) argue that to date, feminist media scholarship has focused more on issues such as the portrayal of women in the mass media, and "how female audience members "read" and respond to messages and images of women" than they have on the structural relations producing women's unfavorable portrayal (p. 2).

Feminist media scholars have always taken up issues of stereotypes and gender socialization, and ideology and pornography. However, Byerly, (quoted. in North, 2006) proposes that "feminist media scholarship needs to move beyond its tendency to be concerned primarily with an analysis of texts and messages and begin to pay more attention to the structural context with which texts are produced and distributed" (p.3). North (2006) added that Byerly's extensive body of feminist research on gendered production practices and newsroom culture has been influential in redirecting feminist media studies scholars from their usual focus on the text to that of production. Many of these feminist media scholars, including Byerly, are former journalists who bring to their research years of personal experience (North, 2006). Byerly, for instance, uses her professional experience as a way of enhancing dialogue between feminist activism and professionalism and therefore has an emancipatory focus (North, 2006). According to Dervin (1987), feminist media scholarship brings a 'female' viewpoint to the field of communication which she contends is 'a new perspective, a new microscope for observation that is not possible of somebody who is in the system. She argues that "women live outside the master's house and therefore cannot use the master's tools for their own articulations" (Dervin, 1987, p.113).

In general, however, feminist media scholarship falls under a broader perspective that explores the meaning of gender in society – feminist studies. The feminist theory is one of those loosely related to the broader critical approach challenging the dominant order of society, as discussed earlier. The essential premise of feminist theory is that many aspects of life are "gendered" – experience in terms of masculine and the feminine. However, they believe that gender is a social construction that is dominated by a male bias and subsequently oppressive to women (Littlejohn, 2002).

Hence, their attempt is to challenge the status quo in society and achieve greater liberation for women. Scholars in this tradition believe that old ways of research coupled with male-biased theories have not only been misleading, but also highly dangerous because they mute the experience of women and hide the values of their experiences. However, in the past 20 years, scholars such as van Zoonen (1994) argue that the founding principles of contemporary western feminism have been dramatically challenged. Others, such as Byerly and Ross (2006), posit that the label feminism itself has undergone considerable scrutiny, argument, and transformation in meaning over the years. They argue that:

> Third world women, women of color, working-class women, and others have debated the work for several decades, questioning whether a term associated with Western (white, bourgeois) origins can legitimately apply to women of other backgrounds and situations. (Byerly & Ross, 2006 p.3)

They cite Mohanty (1991), for instance, who posits that the term *feminism* itself is questioned by many Third World women, arguing that:

> Feminists movements have been challenged on the grounds of cultural imperialism, and of shortsightedness in defining the meaning of gender in terms of middle-class, white experiences, and in terms of internal racism, classism, and homophobia. (Byerly & Ross, 2006 p. 5)

Despite various factors that have led to skepticism and rejection of the label 'feminism' in a number of instances, Mohanty (1991) argues that "third world" women have always engaged with feminism.

The nature of the present study dictates the choice of critical feminist media theory as a primary analytical framework. This is so because the study is concerned with relationships, largely thought to be oppressive of women, with the ambit of the mass media superstructure. Specifically, the study is concerned with the lived experiences of women journalists during and their contributions to the struggle for Namibia's independence. While one recognizes the need for the application of an indigenous African theory to examine this phenomenon, however, in the absence of such Afrocentric theories, one is left with very little choice but to use what may be considered Euro-centric approaches such as the critical feminist media theory, instead.

It is for this reason, therefore, that this study finds it justifiably appropriate to adapt and build on Byerly and Ross's (2006) feminist media theory within an African context. These authors contend that feminist media theory must move beyond its tendency to be concerned primarily with an analysis of texts and messages and begin to pay more attention to the structural context with which texts are produced and distributed. Using the Namibian liberation struggle as a backdrop, the present study analyses the contributions of women journalists in Southern Africa. It aims to answer questions about the experience of women journalists during that period.

5 Literature Review

In order to fully understand the critical role played by women journalists during the Namibian independence struggle, review of the literature on the role of media in the liberation struggle of Namibia becomes necessary. To this end, the purpose of this chapter is to first take a closer look at the literature on the role of the media in the Namibian independence struggle in general, as well as the specific role of women journalist in this liberation effort.

For this reason, available secondary source materials such as books, journal articles, online documents were consulted at libraries in Namibia during the researcher's field trip to Namibia in the summer of 2006. Additionally, an extensive electronic search of other libraries in the United States, including the Library of Congress and the Founder's Library at Howard University, were also made.

The results of these searches have shown that, although there are a few studies that have looked at the role of the media in liberation struggles, there were almost none that explicitly looked at the role and contributions of women journalists, particularly in Namibia, despite the fact that they have played a significant role in that struggle. The absence of scholarly work on the latter serves to reinforce the enormous significance of this present study. This chapter draws on the few studies that were found to be relevant in this examination of the role that women journalists played during Namibia's liberation struggle from 1985–1990. Studies on the role of media in Namibia, South Africa, Algeria, and others are highlighted in this section. Interestingly, the convergence of the role of the media in the liberation struggle on the one hand, and the role of women and women's issues in the media, on the other, has not been extensively studied. This study, therefore, fills the gap in this area of research. A look at some studies by some of the major feminist media scholars such as Byerly and Ross (2004, 2006), Joseph (2004), and North (2006), are also highlighted.

The first section in the Literature Review will highlight research concerning the role of the media in liberation struggles in general. The second section will review relevant literature that discusses the role of women in general in national liberation struggles. The third section will explore the role that women in the media have played in liberation struggles. In accordance with the theoretical framework of this present study, the last section of this chapter looks at some of the relevant literature available on feminist media activism and gender and newsroom culture.

Media in the struggle for liberation

The role of the media has been important in freedom struggles in various ways, most notably in forging a sense of unity among a victimized people, but also by raising awareness through exposing injustices and atrocities and garnering international support to the outside world. World War I, the Vietnam War, the Gulf war, and colonialism serve as instance of how the media can serve as tools to generate popular support against military engagement. However, the media can also play a role that supports the status quo. Switzer (1997) has shown that throughout history, the mainstream media have generally been known for their support for the status quo such as the complicity and backing of colonial regimes. Most mainstream media in colonial Africa tended to support the status quo. The alternative media, on the other hand, tended to agitate for regime change.

Mwase's (1988) work, for example, reveals that during the apartheid era in Namibia, the colonial authorities fully understood the importance of the mass media. Propaganda and information systems were managed from South Africa which consequently controlled the local press. In their study on the way that information was used in the Namibian liberation struggle Sturges et al. (2005) posit that the contest for 'hearts and minds' is more significant than the armed confrontation that accompanies it in liberation struggles. They argue that while South Africa and its Namibian military structures were generally successful in armed confrontation with the People's Liberation Army of Namibia (PLAN), SWAPO's military wing force, they were not able to bring the conflict to a successful military conclusion. This, the authors said, was because SWAPO's focus on diplomacy consisted of strong and consistent information flows to the United Nations and other allies to press for a negotiated and peaceful solution. This is extremely important to note because in an environment which stifled freedom of speech, there was no avenue in which to express one's opinion.

Sturges et al (2005) note that SWAPO's victory was not a conventional military triumph similar to many other successful anti-colonial struggles like those in Malaysia, Kenya and Zimbabwe, where military information campaigns were counterbalanced against aspects of a single struggle. These authors argue that Namibia's information warfare was the most dominant and significant contributor to the independence of Namibia. SWAPO fought the colonial regime at three fronts: diplomatic, political and military.

Obviously, the role of the media has been indispensable in wars dating as far back to those such as World War, to those who fought for the liberation of Namibia, and current wars taking place in the Middle East such as in Iraq. Subsequent searches attempt to establish to what extent the same holds true as it relates to the role of women journalists in the liberation struggle of Namibia in contest.

Women in general in liberation struggles

In his introduction to Frantz Fanon's *A Dying Colonialism,* Adolfo Gilly (1965) illustrates some of the ways women, in general, have been known to have contributed to the liberation struggle. Gilly noted how people that are usually regarded as vulnerable in societies play equally vital roles in revolutions such as the Algerian revolution. Gilly argues that the Algerian revolution shared with other world revolutions (and liberation struggles) certain essential features which he believed could be summed up in the words "mass participation" (Gilly, 1965, p.4). According to Gilly, this means that in a revolution, the women, the family, the children, the aged and everybody else participate. He argues that:

> The double oppression, social and sexual, of the woman cracks and finally shattered; and its essential nature as the social oppression of the family as a whole is revealed. It is simply that its weakest parts – the children, the elderly, the women – must bear the most exaggerated forms of oppression, but in the struggle, the relative weakness, the apparent defenselessness of these groups disappear (Gilly, 1965 p.4).

Gilly explains that, during a revolution, what was formerly a disadvantage becomes an advantage for the revolutionaries. He adds that:

> The old man or woman who walks with halting steps past the military patrol, the timid woman hiding behind veil, the innocent-faced child do not seem to the enemy to be dangers or threats. So they can pass arms, information, medicine. They can prepare surprise attacks, serve as guides and sentries. They can even take up arms themselves. Every sort of cunning is a legitimate weapon to use against the enemy – and an embattled population not composed solely of men but also women, children, and old people (Gilly, 1965, p.4).

This was true even in the liberation struggle of Namibia, in which women, for example, played varying and significant roles. It was also true in all other struggles for emancipation from oppressive structures. Gilly (1965) says women, alongside their male counterparts and other members of the entire family, contributed to exposing or eliminating injustices that had been witnessed, for instance, in Bolivia in the great miners' strikes; in Argentina in the general strikes; in the great struggles of the North American proletariat and so forth. He believes that it is in this kind of struggle that the woman stands firm in her own strength, and throws all the energy she has accumulated over the years of oppression. Fanon (1965) equally shows that women, just like the proletariat, can only truly liberate themselves by liberating all other oppressed strata and sectors of the society, and also by acting together with them.

Women in Zimbabwe have also played a significant role during their country's liberation struggle from the British colony which culminated in that country's independence in 1980. Gann (1981) notes that Zimbabwean women gave up their traditional gender roles of working in agricultural fields and bearing children for their husbands, and instead became equal participants in the guerrilla warfare with their male counterparts.

Since Namibia's independence in 1980, a handful of scholars, have endeavored to investigate the role that women played in that country's liberation struggle. Soiri (1996) examined the role of northern Namibian Ovambo women in the liberation struggle for independence. She chose to study women's contribution to the struggle in this group because they make up the largest ethnic group in Namibia (about 60% of the entire population of the country) and they inhabit an area of the country that was most severely affected by the liberation struggle. In fact, northern Namibia was deemed the war zone during the liberation struggle of the country. She also argued that a study of all Namibian women would be a task for a much wider study.

In choosing her theoretical approach for her study, Soiri (1996) understood that studying women and studying non-western cultures required a perspective that was sensitive to the subject's own concepts and viewpoints different from the traditional approaches that, as argued severally in the present study, tend to be too western. Hence, she uses a combination of approaches offered by Third World feminism, new development theories, and the concepts of nationalism and ethnicity.

Soiri (1996) also acknowledges the fact that when studying women, one is also drawn into the areas of feminism and women's studies which help her in an attempt to examine whether the participation of women could be seen as a women's struggle, motivated by oppression on the basis of their gender and ideas of equality between sexes. However, she argues that societies based on racial strata tend to have an absence of feminism, like it was the case in Namibia.

Soiri (1996) used in-depth interviews and group discussions with 25 Ovambo-speaking women conducted in northern Namibia in early 1994, as well as participant observation and a variety of secondary sources. Her choice of her research methods, particularly in-depth interviews, are deemed by many researchers on societal dynamics in independent Namibia as the best since very few empirical studies could be conducted during the apartheid regime which kept Namibia in exclusion from the outside world.

Ultimately, Soiri (1996) found that Ovambo women have actively participated in the struggle against colonialism since the beginning of the armed struggle against the South African regime. These women played a crucial role in harboring SWAPO members and fighters who would sneak into the country from their bases such as those in neighboring Angola. These women also played a role in providing intelligence to these SWAPO fighters, and assisting with the storage and movement of weaponry around the country. She said women did not only provide food, shelter and moral support to the combatants but also took political initiatives themselves. She cited as an example of one of the mothers in Ovamboland who wrote a letter to the United Nations in 1973 reporting the treatment people were subjected to in the war zone. She aired Namibian women's disgruntlement of giving birth to children who were going to be treated like slaves in their own country of birth and did not have a chance to eat the fruits of their land peacefully. This woman's letter was smuggled out of the country by the missionaries and, according to Soiri (1996), the author's name was blacklisted and she was then forced to leave the country into exile. Soiri's (1996) study also reveals some of the hardships women had to bear, for example, from the 1960s to the independence election in 1989, women in Ovamboland were subject to curfews. Anyone moving outside during the hours of darkness could automatically be shot, and this was particularly a challenge to pregnant women who needed to reach hospital at night to deliver their babies (Soiri, 1996). Women faced a lot of constraints during these years of the struggle and Soiri (1996) argues that it was even more so that at the time, women were not in a position to initiate a common organizational base for their activities, although they used the Church for most of their resistance.

Cooper (1997) reinforces some of the sentiments concluded in Soiri's (1996) study arguing that women in the war zone (mostly Ovambo women) faced hardships unique to their gender. However, like other women elsewhere in the country, they experienced their share of banning, detainments, imprisonment, torture, and death, regardless of their political affiliation.

Prior to Soiri (1996), scholars such as Cleaver and Wallace (1990) also embarked on a study to look at Namibian women's participation in the liberation for independence and freedom. Their book on *Namibia Women in War* was a result of a research visit conducted from April to July 1988. Their visit to Namibia was set up by Church Action on Namibia with the specific aims of gathering background material for their campaigning work to raise awareness generally and among the churches in Britain (Cleaver & Wallace, 1990). Their concern was to gather views and activities of ordinary people, and the ways in which people were managing to organize against the repression. They were interested in learning about women and women's organizations, the unions and British-based companies, churches, and youth groups. In August 1989, one of the authors returned to Namibia from Britain and that experience enabled her to update some of the material.

According to the authors, in writing the book, they confronted the problem of how to present their findings in a manner that Namibian women would recognize as reflecting the realities of their situation among other things. As white middle-class women, the authors point out that they were aware of the dangers involved in writing from a point of view of privilege, relative to the women to whom they were studying. According to Cleaver and Wallace (1990), Namibian women were objects of soldier's brutality. They perceived the war as the root of their every day struggles at the time. Their resistance to the war took on different levels by, according to Cleaver and Wallace, surviving and maintaining social structures in the face of constant onslaught; by active strategies to equip themselves better for this task; by actively supporting the PLAN fighters; and finally, by joining the resistance army themselves as combatants.

In her paper presented at UNIN (United Nations Institute for Namibia) conference, Ginwala (1988) raised some salient issues concerning the role of women in national liberation struggles. She argued that rather than just looking at the question of their role, there was first a need to examine the question of women's oppression and liberation. She questions whether women in national liberation struggles needed to be concerned with the relationship between women's oppression and women's liberation or if they needed to be concerned primarily with looking at the relationship between women's oppression and national liberation (Ginwala, 1988).

However, Ginwala (1988) offered some key thoughts on these salient issues that she said were also being questioned not only within the national liberation movements, but also with the international feminist movements at the time. She believed that to begin to formulate an answer, an examination of the nature of women's oppression under the apartheid system in South Africa and in Namibia was very crucial. She believed that while there was much in common with women's oppression in other societies, the apartheid movement imposed an additional oppression on women that was distinct and was different in content and character from that elsewhere. In her attempt to offer some of the specificity of women's oppression under apartheid, and particularly looking at how women were seen in the context of capitalist society in South Africa and Namibia, Ginwala (1988) further pointed out that these two societies particularly, in the ruling circles, were societies dominated by males. She adds that "even amongst the privileged whites, women are noticeable by their absence in the organs of decision-making" (p.49).

However, she argues that if one compared the situation of white women to black women in both South Africa and Namibia, the white women were privileged and to a degree, free from domestic labor and responsibility. She further argued that although these white women had the franchise and the legal opportunities which would allow them to help shape a more egalitarian society, they did not do it. She further argues that due to the "white privilege" that white women enjoyed during apartheid Namibia, these white women generally also refused to acknowledge the oppression of black women and have generally failed to question their own status (Ginwala, 1988).

However, Ginwala (1988) points out the fact that women were more concerned about their oppression from the apartheid regime as opposed to their oppression by men, and hence turned more attention on the larger struggle for national liberation. But, by the same token, women activists also argued that victory over apartheid would not automatically remove the oppression of women, nor that after national liberation women would begin a new struggle for their own liberation; but rather, it was to say that, for women, the two struggles were intertwined.

Thus far, we have explored some of the ways women in general have played their roles as part of the embattled population in liberation struggles in countries such as Algeria, Zimbabwe and Namibia. One can argue that establishing some of these roles that women are known to have played in these struggles served as a backdrop to this present study as it endeavored to establish the role that women journalists played during the liberation struggle of Namibia's freedom.

Women in the media

The accounts put forth by Pinnock (1997) on the courage of Ruth First are testimony to the role that women journalists played both inside and outside the South African borders. Analyzing First's work, which was written in the context of resistance politics during the 1950s, Pinnock tells of how she left no stone unturned to unveil the atrocities and exploitations that farm laborers, in particular, were subjected to by their colonial masters. First, a journalist with the *Guardian,* a left-wing newspaper, was in the forefront of African women's anti-pass campaigns that were a central issue in South African resistance politics in the 1950s. First exposed the then ravaging poverty in Johannesburg's African townships inflicted upon the Africans by the racist government. She did not only report on these issues, but since she belonged to a journalistic tradition that required its practitioners to be activists, she also began to campaign for better housing, improved living conditions and better living wages for these oppressed people (Pinnock, 1997).

In 1962, this woman journalist hopped into a train from South Africa and headed for Namibia to conduct interviews that culminated into her famous book *South West Africa.* Upon her arrival in Namibia, First was hardly a week in the capital, Windhoek, when words went around the political police that there was an outsider in town, talking to Africans, asking questions, taking notes, and riding about in a car of the Herero Councilors, and asking for government reports in the archives. When she visited the archives, and was allowed to sit and work from there, however, the archivist made it clear he would decide which materials she could have access to. First was therefore forced to conduct her interviews under clandestine circumstances. In *South West Africa*, published in 1963, First reveals the difficulties she faced conducting these interviews while under the surveillance of the security police. She writes that the scrutiny never faltered:

> The trail to the dry cleaner and the shoemaker, the skulking next to the telephone booth, both ends of the road and every exit of the hotel patrolled, detectives following me to the airport, to the post office to buy stamps, watching me at breakfast, interviewing people I had seen – 'what does she want from you?' (p.13).

First (1963) reveals that, people from the African community in Windhoek were eager to talk to her, but police scrutiny made it more and more difficult. She said Africans were now forced to go through interviews with First while glancing over their shoulders. First (1963) recalls that one interviewee, an old man, wrote in a note smuggled into her hotel room that "I know I will be a fugitive when my words are published" (p.14).

This account shows how this courageous female journalist experienced difficulties to undertake her journalistic work in Windhoek in 1962 at a time when there were hardly, or no female journalists at all in the city. Ruth First fought persistently against the suppression of the African people not only of South Africa but also of other countries such as Namibia. She was later forced to flee South Africa into exile, after a series of arrests, jail, and solitary confinement. About 20 years after her 1962 interviews in Namibia, First was killed by a letter bomb planted by the notorious South African security agents, which exploded in her hands in 1982 while in exile in Mozambique.

Herbstein and Evenson (1989) investigated similar problems faced by Namibia's leftist woman journalist, Gwen Lister, who was targeted for assassination by the South African security force in the late 1980s. The formation of Lister's paper, *The Namibian,* was a blessing to oppressed Namibians who yearned for truthful news coverage of the struggle in the country. There were obstacles to the existence of *The Namibian* from the onset. The paper faced its first threat when the interim proxy government appointed by South Africa learned about plans to start a newspaper (Herbstein and Evenson, 1989). A deposit of about $5,000 was levied under the terms of the Newspaper Imprint and Registration Act, claiming that the newspaper and Lister, as its editor, were a threat to the security of the state. But according to Herbstein and Evenson (1989), the paper's lawyers cited the freedom of speech clause in the Bill of Fundamental Rights when challenging the amount of money it was forced to pay as guarantee of 'good behavior'. The court ruled in the favor of *The Namibian*. Despite all this, *The Namibian* picked up a readership of 100,000 and according to Herbestein and Evenson (1989), this readership included the South African army, police, and government who turned to it to find out about public opinion (p.167). As part of continuous attempts to silence Lister and her editorial team, in 1988, a 'mystery bomber' destroyed the paper's offices and equipment. However, that did not discourage them from continuing to publish.

In summary, women journalists, such as Gwen Lister and Ruth First, have indeed played significant roles during the liberation struggles of their respective countries. This information is relevant as this present study attempts to take a closer look at the role of Namibian women journalists in the struggle for their country's independence.

Feminist media activism and gender and newsroom culture

De Bruin and Ross (2004) have also been concerned with investigations of gendered professional practices in the newsroom. Actually, the authors in their edited volume discuss how the male journalist prefers to view his female colleague in terms of her gender before accepting her as a professional; hence, giving an impression that the journalism field was indeed a male preserve. In the introduction to their edited volume, de Bruin and Ross (2004) posit that they made a deliberate effort to include voices that are heard less often in international academic debate, "yet that represent a majority of the world's realities" (p. viii). They explained that sometimes the absence of these voices is caused by their lack of resources to embark on their own research agenda instead of depending on working with an agenda driven by the interests of external funding agencies.

Of particular interest to the present study is Aida Opoku-Mensah's (2004) article which examines and assesses the complexities that surround gender roles and responsibilities in societies. Opoku-Mensah (2004) posits that understanding gender analyses in the African continent is a relatively new concept that began in 1994 when it became obvious that development strategies had not adequately addressed women's access and control over economic resources, and therefore had failed to account for women's contributions to national economies. She adds that "Subsequently, gender analyses became a useful tool for different groups, particularly those working in civil society, although it is still a relatively new concept in the media and communication field" (Opoku-Mensah, 2004, p.105). Opoku-Mensah (2004) highlights the fact that women are still deprived top managerial positions in male-dominated newsrooms in Africa.

However, Opoku-Mensah's (2004) concern about gendered professional practices in African newsrooms was beyond the numbers. She questioned issues such as how social and traditional norms are replicated in newsrooms and how they define the power relations between female and male media workers. She questions whether women are free to pursue a career in journalism in the same way as men, and whether women are free to cover the same stories as men. She argues that these questions are useful in trying to determine how women journalists themselves feel about their roles and responsibilities. She further argue however, that there are no real definitions of what constitutes gender relations within the context of African newsrooms because this area of research is still in its infancy or underdeveloped. Opoku-Mensah (2004) posits that:

> The examination of the relative positions of men and women in newsrooms and the division of roles, responsibilities, benefits, rights, power, and privilege have so far been anecdotal and have not been documented in any systematic way. The socio-cultural factors that inhibit women in their lives as journalists have often not been discussed in relation to the power dynamics that exist in newsrooms across the continent (Opoku-Mensah, 2004, p.106).

Through the testimonies of both women and men, journalists themselves, Opoku-Mensah (2004) examines the persistence of the male-female divide and "its translation into socio-legal and socio-cultural media practice that produces a culture of discrimination and bias, characterized by inequity and inequality in all aspects of media work" (p. 106). Opoku-Mensah (2004) asserts that there is a dearth of information and research on media and gender issues in Africa. She conducted a study to verify the general belief that women often work in "hostile" working environments in journalism. Her study was among practitioners (both men and women) on their experiences of working in newsrooms in five African countries (Ghana, Kenya, Zimbabwe, Lesotho, and Zambia). The women interviewed working in newsrooms reported that they are often confronted with a mindset based on the current social and traditional norms that prevail in many African societies – a mindset that Opoku-Mensah said, results in stereotypical attitudes, such as the persistent perception that women are the weaker sex, are poor performers, and lack depth, that hamper women's professional development. Despite the unavailability of detailed research on male attitudes toward female colleagues in newsrooms, Opoku-Mensah's (2004) study indicated that male reporters harbor stereotypical notion of women in general that derive from the wider society. Also, it is a well-known fact that the field of journalism in Africa is perceived as a male preserve. Media activism has been an integral part of modern social change processes throughout the world. In their study on women and media activism, Byerly and Ross (2006) researched the relationship of feminist media activists to feminist movements, reporting that two-thirds of the 90 participants they interviewed in 20 different nations had indicated that their media activism involved using print or broadcast media in some way. The authors defined women's media activism as "any organized effort on women's part to make changes in established media enterprises or to create new structures with the goal of expanding women's voice in society and enabling their social advancement" (p.101). These media they were concerned with encompassed both traditional, which is mainstream, commercial media, as well as nontraditional, which is independent audience-specific media. Broadcast media included radio and television, (p. 110). Women activists used these outlets to air their voices in a bid to gain visibility.

In their study, Byerly and Ross (2006) offer a Model of Women's Media Action (MWMA) in order to better theorize the ways in which women's media activism functions in women's liberation movements. They demonstrate that women's media activism can be organized into four main paths or approaches. They term the first path *politics to media,* which *is* represented by feminists who decide to use the media as part of their work. The second path, *media profession to politics,* refers to when women who are employed in the media and decide to use their vantage point as insiders to expand women-related content or to reform the industry's policies to improve women's professional status. The third path, *advocate change agent,* is followed by women who pressure media to improve the treatment of women in one or more ways through outside campaign. And the fourth path, *women's media enterprises,* gives women the maximum control over message production and distribution (Byerly & Ross, 2006, p.127).

Analysis of the findings of this present study have particularly benefited from some elements of the second and fourth paths of Byerly and Ross's (2006) Model of Women's Media Action. For example, the second path – *media profession to politics* – relates to this present study because women who followed that path, according to Byerly and Ross (2006), are media professionals who were formally trained in the media profession such as news reporting, radio or television production, or some other kind of media work who used their presence in the media to advance women's issues. These women use their employment in the media to keep women informed about their rights in usually male-dominated environments.

The fourth path – *women's media enterprises* – is relevant to the present study because it represents women who establish their own media and use those outlets to advocate for gender equities. Owning their own media outlets allows these women to exercise uninhibited control over the contents they produce and subsequently their distribution (Byerly & Ross, 2006).

Byerly's (2004) earlier work examined the women-and-news relationship, and in the process, she explores masculine newsroom hegemony, reviews the feminist critique of news, summarizes numerous examples of feminist news interventions, and explores why these matter in relation to a women's right to communicate. Byerly's academic concern with a women's relationship to news and other media is grounded in her years as a journalist, public relations professional, activist, and academic. These collective experiences have taught her that "women will never gain full social participation or political power until they are able to speak about women's concerns, indeed all matters of public interests, in the mainstream news of their nations" (Byerly, 2004, p.110). This consideration is especially important in the context of this study because it underlines the pivotal importance of women's participation in the media.

Byerly (2004) posits that feminist criticism of the news can be organized under three main problems. The first, she argues, focuses on women's absence in most serious news content. She said, "such invisibility has the effect of reinforcing women's marginality through what Tuchman (1978a) called a 'symbolic annihilation of women'." She adds that, women as relevant and accomplished social actors continue to be unknown and their absence from routine information purveyed by news media don't seem to matter when they are not heard or seen (Byerly, 2004). The second problem she posits has been one of representation, or portrayal. She argues that in an event when women are included in news media, they are either misrepresented or distorted by, for example, focusing on their sexual attributes as women and ignoring ideas, activities, and accomplishments. She believes that women intellectualism is portrayed in most cases as inferior to that of their male counterparts; or they are even shown in their traditional private sphere roles of mother, wife, sister, caretaker, or servant downplaying their more complex identities. The third problem Byerly posits is one of access to the news-making apparatus. Posing that the main issue of concern here have been women's employment and advancement within the news industry where news is defined, formulated, and distributed (Byerly, 2004).

Byerly's (2004) study also highlights the fact that news corporations in the United States, for example, are almost exclusively the domains of very wealthy white men, and women's involvement in the news industry is at a very small scale and along with persons of non-European heritage, they are hardly employed above the journalistic ranks.

Another problem she raises is the issue of masculine newsroom hegemony which is accomplished not through explicit exercise of overt authoritarian control by those in charge that are usually men, but rather through institutionalized hiring and promotional practices that, she claims, privilege white men. Newsroom hegemony, she said, is manifested in determining which events should be covered and from what angle or perspective, and which facts and sources should be included in a story (Byerly, 2004).

However, Byerly (2004) believes that feminist action to change the situation has been longstanding, both in the US and around the world. She posits that women have utilized a variety of feminist news interventions to interrupt prevailing sexist policies or practices in news making or framing and to repeal them with policies and practices more are more inclusive and favorable of women. Byerly divides these interventions into categories of external and internal campaigns. She defines external campaigns as interventions led by independent advocacy groups that lodge particular complaints about treatment of women, or advocacy groups that engage in strategic activism of some sort. While internal campaigns, she posits, are those waged within newsrooms by journalists themselves, often with support from their professional organizations and labor unions.

Byerly (2004) posits that around the world, women have employed a range of external intervention campaigns citing as example of the Women Media Watch organization (WMW) in Jamaica which has been in the forefront of a campaign to clean-up the image of women in that country's media. Since its establishment in 1987, WMW have been concerned with the portrayal of violence against women, or women as sex objects. WMW members use a non-confrontational approach, meeting with media managers and basically encouraging them to look at their work from a gender perspective (Byerly, 2004).

Another example of external intervention that Byerly (2004) cited is that of the joint efforts by both women and men's groups in Zimbabwe that work together to address the problem of women's media representation. She posits that these efforts include holding workshops and other meetings for male journalists to create the sensitivity of women issues.

Meanwhile, other scholars such as Joseph (2004), North (2004), Aida Opoku-Mensah (2004) and de Bruin and Ross (2004) have also conducted studies on newsroom cultures in India, Australia, Africa, the United Kingdom and in the U.S. In their respective studies, they aimed at "unmasking the macho newsroom" practices. Their studies have indicated that "masculine newsroom hegemony" remain pervasive in many newsrooms globally.

Joseph (2004) attempts to describe the complex reality of the media and women in India. She highlights some issues concerning access, employment, and decision making through examples from different sections of the media in her vast home country – India. In this study, Joseph (2004) states that, although there has been some progress over the years, women's participation in and access to the media, and its impact on the use as instrument for the advancement and empowerment of women, remain something that requires improvement. Also, North (2004) examines negotiations over feminism in a series of dialogues that occurred in the newsroom where she worked as a subeditor at *The Mercury* newspaper in Hobart, Australia. Her study is concerned with how feminism and ideas of feminism are deployed in the newsroom. Her discussions with her colleagues centered on the publication of an image of a group of female anti-war protesters who protested while naked. These acts of women activism resonate with this study's contention that women all over the world have been known for their pivotal roles in social change.

In essence, what the reviewed literature conducted in this chapter has indicated, among other things, is that women work under less than ideal conditions in their bid to execute their duties as journalists as compared, for example, with their male counterparts. Furthermore, the literature also suggests that while women in general did play equally important roles in the liberation struggles of many countries, however, these roles have not been fully highlighted nor extensively recognized by scholars. Therefore, the current study is an attempt to fill in some of this gap, especially as it relates to the role in the liberation struggle of Namibia was concerned.

In the next chapter, the research designed adopted for the study is discussed. In other words, the chapter explains the qualitative approach that informs the study, the interview method used to collect the data, the type of sample used, the process by which participants were selected, how the data analysis was conducted, as well as why the qualitative method was found to be appropriate for the study.

6 Methodology, Research and Participants

This study is an attempt to determine the extent to which women journalists in Namibia contributed to the liberation struggle for the independence of the country and how their gender and race affected their ability to execute their roles. Information was collected onsite in Namibia from both primary and secondary sources. Primary sources such as interviews in the context of oral histories were used to collect information from 13 women who worked as reporters from 1985 to 1990 in media organizations (newspapers, television and radio, and even at a newsletter of the Council of Churches in Namibia [CCN]) that existed at the time in the country. This researcher has used face-to-face interviews in the context of Oral History to obtain answers to the three research questions of this present study:

1. What constraints, if any, did Namibian women journalists confront in their news organizations during the liberation years?
2. How did women deal with these constraints during that era?
3. What do they identify as their contributions to the liberation struggle of the country?

Qualitative research as an approach

Qualitative research is one of the two major approaches to research methodology in social sciences. It focuses on meaning-making by humans. In other words, it involves an in-depth understanding of human behavior and the reasons that govern human behavior. Unlike quantitative researchers, qualitative researchers seek to preserve and analyze the situation from, content, and experience of social action, rather than subject it to mathematical or other formal transformations (Potter, 1996; Denzin & Lincoln, 2000; Lindlof & Tylor, 2002). These authors posit that qualitative research investigates, for example, the why and how of decision making, as compared to what, where, and when of quantitative research. It focuses more on smaller samples as opposed to the usual practice in quantitative research that tend to focus more on large, random samples. The qualitative approach categorizes research data into patterns as the primary basis for organizing and reporting results (Potter, 1996; Denzin & Lincoln, 2000; Lindlof & Tylor, 2002). According to Lindlof and Taylor, actual talk, gesture, just to name a few, are the raw materials of analysis. These authors add that many qualitative studies eschew participant observation and are based solely on interview data. In fact, according to Lindlof and Taylor, studies using qualitative methods often focus only on a partial set of relationships in a scene. For example, this present study's focus is on the contribution that Namibian women journalists made to the liberation struggle while operating in a male-dominant environment.

The interview as a qualitative research method

Potter (1996) defines interviewing as a technique of gathering data from humans by asking them questions and getting them to react verbally. It is a face-to-face interpersonal situation where an interviewer asks questions of another – the respondent (Potter, 1996). Potter (1996) adds that in interviews, questions are designed to obtain answers pertinent to a particular research problem. There are several ways of characterizing interviews: they can be structured or unstructured, casual or in-depth, standardized or unstandardized (Denzin & Lincoln, 2002; Potter, 1996). According to these authors, in the standardized interview, the questions are predetermined by the interviewer while in unstandardised interviews, they are less structured. Marshall and Rossman (1989) add that typically, qualitative in-depth interviews are more like conversations than the formal structured ones. In these in-depth interviews, the researcher explores a few wide-range topics in a bid to uncover the participant's meaning perspective, but however, respects how the participant frames and structures the responses (Marshall & Rossman, 1989). Meanwhile, Kerlinger and Lee (2000) described the interview as the most ubiquitous method of obtaining information from people. His sentiments were shared by Fontana and Frey (2002) who posit that:

> The spoken or written word has always a residue of ambiguity, no matter how carefully we word the questions and how carefully we report or code the answers. Yet interviewing is one of the most common and powerful ways in which we try to understand our fellow human beings (Fontana & Frey, 2002, p.645).

Kerlinger and Lee (2000) also point out that the interview is probably one of the oldest and most used technique for obtaining information. They note that the interview has important qualities that objective tests and scales and behavioral observations do not possess. When used properly, with for instance a well conceived schedule, Kerlinger and Lee (2000) claim that it can obtain a great deal of information. It is also flexible and easily adaptable to individual situations, and can be used when no other method is possible or adequate. For instance, interviews particularly played a major role to this present study because there were no other adequate methods that were perceived to provide data that could give us a picture of the contributions that Namibian women journalists made to the liberation struggle, as well as information on how they fared in newsrooms that were perceived male domains.

The interviewing approach is also popular among feminist media scholars who use it to study newsroom cultures. Feminist media scholars such as North (2006) have used interviews in her exploration of the gendered production of news, and in particular the experiences of women in the Australian print media. In her study *The Gendered Newsroom: Embodied Subjectivity in the Changing World of Media,* North conducted more than a dozen in-depth, semi-structured interviews with both male and female journalists working in the Australian print news media around the year 2004. Through the interviewing technique, North (2002) was about to elicit information from her participants on issues of concern to her study such as how newsroom culture in Australia was embodied, what were the discourses of sexually harassing behavior in the newsroom, and other issues such as how feminism was played out in the newsroom.

Similarly, the qualitative in-depth interviews were also found to be more appropriate in this present study as opposed to other forms such as ethnographic interviews which involve observing the journalist at her worksite over time and considering a complex environment along with her interview statements. This was so because, as indicated earlier, in-depth interviews are much more like conversations than formal, structured interviews. In in-depth interviews, the researcher explores a few general topics to help uncover the participant's meaning perspective, but otherwise respects how the participant frames and structures the responses (Potter, 1996). On the other hand, ethnographic interview differs from friendly interviews in ways such as the fact that it is not balanced as much as most conversations are. Instead, the ethnographer informs the interviewee of the purpose of the interview and then takes control by asking questions and probing the person's responses. This type of interviewing, according to Potter (1996), is structured like survey interviewing; the key difference is that it is responsive to situations rather than standardized. "Nondirective questions are open-ended and designed to get the interviewee talking about a broad topic area" (Potter, 1996, p.97).

Selection of participants

Having worked as a woman journalist in Namibia, albeit after the liberation struggle, this researcher did not encounter much trouble to locate these women to participate in the study. Hence, to ensure that the research had a complete list of all the women who worked as journalists during the study timeframe, a 'snowballing' method was used to recruit participants. Qualitative researchers believe that this technique is the most efficient and productive way of recruiting a heterogeneous group of participants. Initially, for the present study, the researcher composed a list of women journalists she could remember who worked during the period under investigation. This list was circulated to potential interviewees and to other journalists, both female and male, who did not necessarily work as reporters during the study period but were deemed knowledgeable as to who worked during that period.

According to Potter (1996), snowballing is a popular technique used in generating a purposive sample. He explains that this technique begins as a purposive sample where the researcher finds people to interview who could provide him or her with important insights. Potter (1996) explains that during the interview, the researcher asks for names of additional people to talk with – thereby expanding the initial list of interviewees. By using this technique, the interviewer starts out with a small list but gathers momentum and weight as the research proceeds. In other words, the technique yields its study sample through referrals made among a group of people who know of others who possess some characteristics that are of research interest (Lindlof & Taylor, 2002). Feminist scholars such as North (2006) used a snowball technique that began with her contacting a few people in the Australian media industry, and hence, through a series of referrals, she ended up interviewing seventeen media workers for her study on the gendered production of news in the Australian print media as mentioned earlier.

Therefore, the "snowballing method" was found to be the most pragmatic to acquire information for the present study. Although this process provided 16 women who were deemed to have worked during the period of liberation, this researcher interviewed only 13 of them for reasons explained in the following section. Therefore, these participants likely comprise almost 100% of the population. The project was approved by the Howard University's Institutional Review Board (IRB) in June 2006 and the field study was aided on-site in Namibia by cooperating faculty member, Mr. Graham Hopwood, a lecturer in the department of Media and Technology at the Polytechnic of Namibia. Mr. Hopwood also assisted the researcher in locating journalists and guided this researcher on some relevant information and material that was deemed useful to the study.

During and after the snowballing process, these participants were provided with a statement (via e-mail) explaining the goals of the research and a list of questions was attached to prepare them for face-to face interviews. In the case of electronic interviews, responses to those questions were e-mailed back to the researcher. Interviewees were also provided with a statement explaining their rights as research subjects. This statement informed them of the researcher's intent to publish their names and organizations in the researcher's doctoral dissertation and any other publications that might result from the dissertation. The present book was born out of that dissertation. However, only one out of the 13 participants requested anonymity.

Meanwhile, these female journalists were asked questions such as what gender-related constraints they faced as women journalists in their news organizations during the liberation years; what their assignments were and whether they were assigned stories based on the fact that they are women or whether they had liberty to report on any assignments regardless of their gender as women; whether as women journalists they made any efforts to cover women and women's issues in their stories and what criteria they used. Women were also asked about how blatant, if any, gender inequality was in Namibia's media institutions during the struggle, and the sort of obstacles women journalists encountered in an attempt to get decision-making responsibilities in media organizations, if there were any. The researcher was also interested in establishing, among other things, whether there was an organized feminist agenda in the Namibian newsrooms at the time, and many other questions that were deemed important to give light to the three research questions (mentioned earlier in this book) of this present study.

These questions aimed to get first hand information about how women journalists fared at the time in a male-dominated media and in an apartheid system. Issues of sexism and discrimination against women were explored to determine whether they existed or not, without losing the main thrust of the study.

Procedures

These 13 women were subjected to in-depth, semi-structured interviews. Nine of the interviews were conducted face-to-face in the Namibian capital, Windhoek in the summer (July to August) of 2006. These interviews took place at either interviewee's workplaces in a private room, or at their homes, cafes or over dinner in a restaurant. The face-to-face interviews took approximately an hour and were recorded. They were later transcribed verbatim (see the Appendix), and then subjected to qualitative analyses (see Chapter IV). The latter entailed the use of coding tools designed to derive descriptive statistical data about participants' roles, goals, and perceived contributions of their work during the liberation struggle, and other topical areas suggested by the research questions (see also the Appendix).

Four of the interviews were conducted electronically via e-mail to accommodate scheduling conflicts. Some of the female journalists who worked during the period under study have since relocated to South Africa. However, although the researcher traveled to South Africa to interview the two female journalists there, it was impossible to meet with either of them for a face-to-face interview.

Profile of participants

Women journalists who worked during that era were not necessarily indigenous Namibians. Most of them were white women and born in South Africa, but the majority are now Namibian citizens. In fact, only three out of the 13 women interviewed were black and indigenous Namibians. As mentioned earlier, by authors Lush (1989) and Mwase (1988), there were virtually no black Namibian journalists inside the country at the time, let alone women, due to the apartheid system that made it impossible for black people, especially women, to venture into more perceived prestigious fields such as journalism. Apart from the substandard Bantu education that did not quite prepare the majority of black people in apartheid Namibia to take up professions such as journalism. Some black people (particularly women) did not even bother to apply for jobs in industries such as the media because they perceived them to be "white only" institutions.

Data analysis

The researcher constructed a coding sheet comprising categories that emerged from issues raised by the interview questions of this present study. These categories include gender constraints, political constraints, race constraints, resistance, acceptance, avoidance, racial equality and justice, and gender equality. These categories generated sub-themes from the interviews, such as being black-listed by the government, government intimidation, death threats, male-female conflicts, gender exploitation, lack of opportunities in the decision-making process (glass-ceiling), lack of promotions, absence of gender consciousness in the newsrooms, lack of support for black women journalists, marginalization of those who were considered as 'sell-outs' (by their racial group), official government harassment, and so forth.

Analysis of the narratives of the women journalists interviewed for this present study focused on their role and contribution to the liberation struggle and on how they fared in a male-dominated media industry. This study does not quite suggest that these interviewees' narratives and discussions with this researcher can be understood as objective "truth", but it is understood as part of their individual "truth".

Reliability and validity of the qualitative study design

Reliability and validity are the two concepts that speak to the credibility of the research findings. Reliability is described as the extent to which a technique applied repeatedly to the same object would yield the same result each time, while validity in qualitative research has to do with description and explanation and whether or not the explanation fits the description (Denzin & Lincoln, 2002; Lindlof & Taylor, 2002; Potter, 1996). Validity is concerned with whether the explanation is credible. Denzin and Lincoln (2002) posit that qualitative researchers do not however claim that there is only one way of interpreting an event, or in other words, there is no one "correct" interpretation.

In the present study, the interview method inherently relies on self-reported data and therefore is guided by what is important to the subjects. For example the women journalists interviewed may not have perceived their role in the context of a male dominated environment, therefore not necessarily recognizing the feminist media activism in which they may have been a part. Sampling likely did not introduce bias as almost 100% of the population was studied. Nonetheless, to the extent to which the three remaining journalists had unique perspectives, some bias may be present.

Secondary sources

Books, journals, magazines, archives, newspapers, newsletters, websites, and other relevant documents were consulted as secondary sources of information for this study. These documents were located at facilities such as the Founders Library at Howard University and the Library of Congress in Washington, DC; the National Library, the National Archives, and the Library of the University of Namibia (UNAM) in Windhoek, Namibia. The researcher was particularly aware of the unreliability of certain online Internet material and extra care was taken in the use of such sources. These documents basically provided background information for this study and enriched the literature review section. All sources are cited.

Operational definitions of terms

In the context of this study, several operational terms require a thorough definition and explanation. In this book, women journalists shall be defined as women – white, black, and colored (i.e., mixed race) – who worked as reporters, sub-editors, editors, freelance writers, or those who held other strategic positions in print and electronic media. Namibian liberation struggle will refer to the armed struggle, from 1966 to 1990, by the South West Africa People's Organization (SWAPO) against South African apartheid rule in Namibia. Gender inequality and sexism shall be defined as prejudice or discrimination based on gender, i.e., women who are considered weaker and less capable than their male counterparts because of their gender. Independent Press is defined in the context of "independence" from a given government and not from political, commercial and other interests. Feminism is defined as the philosophy associated with women's movements that seeks to attain equal rights with men in a nation for example divided by race, ethnicity, class, political affiliation, geography, and historical experience. Underlying, feminism is the belief that society is disadvantageous to women, systematically depriving them of individual choice, political power, economic opportunity and intellectual recognition. Women's media activism is defined as an attempt by grassroots activists to promote alternative media not supported by mainstream news. It is also an organized effort on women's part to make changes in established media organizations or to create new media structures with the goal of expanding women's voice in society and enabling their social advancement. It also includes women's establishment of their own media enterprises.

7 Women Journalists in the Struggle: Gender Constraints

The following chapters present the findings from the analysis of transcripts and written responses from 13 interviews conducted, thus providing an elaboration of the various ways in which Namibian women journalists have contributed to the liberation struggle for the independence of the country, and how they fared in male-dominated newsrooms in an apartheid environment.

Some major categories emerged from issues raised by the interview questions of this present study. These categories were gender constraints, political constraints, race constrains, resistance; acceptance; avoidance; racial equality and justice, and gender equality. These categories further generated sub-themes from the interviews, including such issues as women having to work harder than their male colleagues if they were to be recognized, lack of promotions and hostile work environment, being black-listed by the government, government intimidation, death threats, male-female conflicts, gender exploitation, lack of opportunities in the decision making process, lack of promotions, and the absence of gender consciousness in the newsrooms, the lack of support for black women journalists, marginalization of those who were considered as 'sell-outs' by their racial group, and official government harassment. What follows is therefore a comprehensive data analysis presentation according to the categories identified above.

Research Question One asks: What gender and race-related constraints, if any, did Namibian women journalists confront in their news organizations during the liberation years? This question sought to identify gender, race and political constraints.

All types of obstacles confronted by the female journalists interviewed for the study because of their identity as women are put under the category of gender constraints. These include, for example, the fact that they were paid lower salaries than their male counterparts, given trivial assignments to cover as well as being marginalized from the decision-making process. The purpose of this chapter is to explain these themes that emanated from the gender constraints in details.

Women had to work harder

Gwen Lister, the editor of *The Namibian,* for instance, recalled that, the fact that she wanted to become a political reporter stunned her then editor at the *Windhoek Observer*.

"My editor believed women belonged in the kitchen. But I was insistent and he, in turn, gave me a baptism of fire, the likes of which would have caused most men to flee."

Lister said that she started to work in the early hours of the morning until late at night. Adding that "I was given a huge range of tasks-undoubtedly an attempt on the part of the Editor to 'break' me and prove his point that women couldn't do the job." However, she believes that, the huge range of tasks given to her, although daunting, did help to prepare her with all the skills she needed to start her own newspaper years down the line.

Another interviewee, who preferred anonymity, and thus assigned a pseudonym, Lucy, for the purpose of this study, said she had to work harder and longer hours than most of her male colleagues. She said: "I had to work harder and longer hours to prove myself, to myself, my colleagues and my bosses even though they never said they required or expected that of me." Lucy was a reporter at the then South West Africa Broadcasting Corporation (SWABC), which became the Namibian Broadcasting Corporation (NBC) after independence.

René Lötter, who also worked at SWABC, said: "You had to put your foot down and speak up if you wanted to be taken seriously. Women were expected to be seen and not heard, subservient." She further believes that young pretty women in newsrooms, particularly at SWABC were almost treated as decoration, just to be there and admired by the men and allowing men to downplay and or even not see them as equally capable of being fully-fledged journalists like their male counterparts. Lötter added that:

> Only if you were aligned with a man via marriage or if your dad was a powerful figure you would get more esteem. So if you wanted to be heard during office meetings instead of getting blank stares, you had to state your case clearly and assertively. The girls in the office knew Margaret Thatcher was politically not kosher at the time but boy did we try and emulate her style when dealing with the big boys.

Lötter's sentiments were shared by other interviewees such as Sarah Damases, who worked for *The Namibian,* who argued that during the apartheid era the lives of women journalists were almost trivialized and hence women were almost invisible and they lacked access to what Jürgen Habermas (1984) identified as the democratic public sphere, the social spaces where ideas are posed, exchanged, and debated, and where ideas for cultural and public policy changes take shape.

Although the apartheid system did not allow for a vibrant democratic public sphere in Namibia in general as envisioned by Habermas, however, even the little that existed was one that privileged men rather than women. According to the participants of this study, they, as women, did not have an organised body under which they could rally together in order to share ideas as women journalists or discuss their grievances in those newsrooms regarding the constraints that they faced as women journalists. From this, therefore, one could clearly observe consistent patterns of constraints that were beginning to emerge from the experiences of these women journalists.

Lack of promotions, hostile work environment

Women were also discriminated against in terms of salary. According to Rianne Selle, who worked at several media outlets such as *The Windhoek Advertiser*, during the apartheid era, she left a newspaper because her male colleagues got financial raises and were promoted and she believes she wasn't promoted because she was a woman. She joined another paper and she left again a year later because of the unpleasant male attitude towards women, and was therefore forced to join the private sector. Similarly, Lötter said that men who got married and started families were blatantly promoted (jumped) past their female colleagues with more experience and skills.

'Soft' news for women, 'hard' news for men

Feminist media scholars such as Byerly and Ross (2004), de Bruin and Ross (2004), North (2006), Opoku-Mensah (2004) and Joseph (2004) have all written about the discrimination and frustrations women in newsrooms all over the world suffer as far as news coverage assignments in newsrooms are concerned. Newsroom editors often reserve assignments of 'soft' news for women, and 'hard' news for men. Women journalists that were interviewed for this present study have said that there were very few women journalists during the years of the struggle who did anything more than 'soft' news. Lister, for instance, said that at the time, women were simply not considered for 'dangerous' work which "was the almost exclusive preserve of men, except for those women like myself, who started their own media, and I don't think there were any others, apart from myself, in Namibia at the time".

Lucy remembered how her male colleagues suggested that she cover the First Lady's 'tea parties' and women's meetings, which she adamantly refused. However, she says she was struck by the fact that not many female journalists either desired or fought to cover the male-dominated beats of politics and economics, and also that the male editors didn't actively encourage more women to embrace these subjects.

Lötter also noted that women in the field covering "tough assignments" were in the minority. Women were mainly desk-bound subs and presenters. And according to Estelle de Bruyn, who also worked at SWABC, initially the only journalists who did politics were men who didn't think women could really understand politics. Jo Rogge, who initially worked in the printing industry before she co-founded a women's magazine, *Sister Namibia* in 1989, noted that women were not sent out on hard news stories; there were very few women journalists at the time who did anything more than 'soft' news. Meanwhile, Estelle Coetzee, who co-founded *Sister Namibia* with Rogge, recalls that when she started working as a reporter at a newspaper, it was generally accepted that male cub reporters got the 'male' assignments (police beat, crime beat, court beat – women could tackle the lower courts) and only if you were really intent on 'making it in a male world,' could you access it.

Such experiences of gender imbalances, discrimination, or marginalization of women force women journalists to follow Byerly and Ross's (2006) second path of the Model of Women's Media Action (MWMA) by honing their feminist consciousness. The second path of this model, as mentioned in chapter two of this book, was followed by women who were employed in the media industries and decided to use their vantage point as insiders to expand women-related content or even reform the industry's policies to improve women's professional status. It must, however, be clarified here that the women journalists who worked in Namibia during the period of study may not have understood their work regarding the media as being activist (i.e. social-change oriented) though the majority of them did. Hence, this study has identified some women like Anna Erastus, who wrote a column on women for the *Times of Namibia*, Lucy, Theodora Nandjaa, who was a reporter with the Council of Churches in Namibia's (CCN) newsletter, and Rogge, just to name a few, who could be characterized as women who followed Byerly and Ross's (2006) second path of the Model of Women's Media Action. For instance, Erastus used her presence in the media to address women's issues through the column she initiated; Lucy went out of her way and injected in her work as a journalist women issues, perhaps not explicitly, but she also sought for women interviewees.

However, during interviews with these women journalists in Namibia, one was left with an impression that these women tried to keep a distance from any reference or association with the term 'feminism'. In fact, Carol Kotze, who was editor at the *Times of Namibia,* made it clear to this researcher during the face-to-face interview that she was not a feminist and therefore would not answer any question that related to feminism. These journalists tended to shy away from the concept probably because of the negative connotation associated with it. Mohanty (1991) observed that the term feminism has been questioned by Third World women because of its mostly white western capitalist origin, which some African women have argued cannot be legitimately applicable to themselves. However, Mohanty (1991) has argued that despite the skepticism and rejection of the label 'feminism' in a number of instances, Third World women have always engaged with feminism. It is, therefore, sufficient to argue that some of the women journalists interviewed for this study had a feminist consciousness. A feminist, according to Byerly and Ross (2006), can be understood as someone who takes an active part in social movements through which women in various times and places seek not only to obtain their equal rights with men, but also the ability to enter into public deliberation, institution-building, and other processes associated with citizenship.

In fact, in 1989, Rogge and Coetzee made their women's media activism explicit by founding a feminist publication, *Sister Namibia*. The content of this magazine was devoted to gender issues; carrying issues such as teenage pregnancies and sex education, literacy, health issues, labor issues, women's rights and struggles, women in politics, rural women and issues of domestic violence against women (Heuva, 2001). In fact, because of this magazine's role (*Sister Namibia*) in advancing women's causes, it has essentially become what one could call a 'feminist public sphere' for the Namibian women. According to Byerly and Ross (2006), the feminist public sphere is a:

> feminist communicative space in which women articulate their experiences in their own voices, critique gender inequality, advocate for women's advancement, and identify related social concerns that are often inseparable from gender (eg., race, class, and ethnic) inequality. (p. 116)

Still on the issue of "soft news" for women problem, Damases said when it came to stories that had value they were always assigned to men. Although she worked in a newspaper owned by a woman (Lister), Damases felt discriminated against when her editor dished out assignments for news stories. She recalled that if, for instance, there were two political rallies going on, a male colleague would be assigned to the rally of the party that was perceived most significant such as SWAPO which was the leading party during the election process that led to the country's independence in 1990. And she felt that because she would be assigned to cover a rally of a less significant or less popular political party. Alternatively, she said, she would be assigned on a story that was considered significant only in a company of her male colleagues. But even then, she pointed out, whatever she added to the story was not valued, even if in some instances she was the one who brought the scoop to the newsroom. "Basically there was a lot of discrimination at that time, if one can put it that way," Damases said.

However, women journalists such as Carmen Honey, who worked at newspapers such as *The Windhoek Advertiser* and *The Observer* at the time, said she did not generally feel discriminated against as a female journalist during the liberation era. The only time she recalls that she somehow felt discriminated against was when she was denied on mission to go into a government warship to cover an aftermath of a battle between the apartheid regime and the PLAN fighters at a war zone in Angola because she was a woman. Kotze had a different take on this. She said that her male colleagues did not treat her as a woman because she didn't insist on being treated as a woman. She said:

> I became one of the boys. Meanwhile, the Afrikaans[1] women [Kotze was from the British Namibian community] were treated as women. They were sent on news assignments such as to cover the flower shows, women stories, which I am not slightly interested in… the cancer's association tea parties for instance or welfare and other things like that.

Kotze said during her days as a reporter at a news organization in the country, she was an agricultural reporter, a strictly male job at the time. She emphasized. "I use to drive around the country to all the agricultural shows; I had to interview the farmers. I became quite an expert in agriculture, which is a male job," she said. She also worked as a crime reporter. "I had to go to all the murder scenes, suicides and things like that." Kotze was also once a military correspondent when she worked for *Die Republikein* newspaper at one point, covering the war. Once, she recalls, the newspaper sent her to cover the aftermath of a battle that had just taken place between SWAPO soldiers and the South West Africa Territory Force (SWATF) in neighboring Angola. "The military flew us from Windhoek in a Dakota into Angola," she said. However, Kotze believes that the difference between her and most of the women in the newsrooms in the country at the time was that she was educated. That, she said, made a difference. Kotze believes that by the time she went into journalism in the 1960s, she was already well educated as compared to other people in the journalism field at the time in Namibia. Although not formally trained in the field of journalism, Kotze said she earned a BA degree in English and history at the University of Pretoria. She later furthered her studies in the field through the University of South Africa, a distance education university, where she earned master's and doctoral degrees.

Another constraint faced by some women such as Rogge was the fact that her media organization at the time did not allow women journalists to travel out of the capital, Windhoek, without male colleagues when required to go out of the city to do their media-related duties.

The glass ceiling

The glass ceiling effect is whereby women "make steady progress as entrants into the sector but then do not go on to achieve senior positions" (Byerly & Ross, 2006, p. 77). Female

---

[1] Afrikaners are white South Africans of predominantly Calvinist Dutch, German, French Huguenot, Friesian and Walloon descent who speak Afrikaans.

journalists also suffered discrimination when it came to promotions to decision-making position. According to Lister, there were few or no women in decision making in media at that time. Lister said that, "I would not have had such power if I hadn't created the position for myself by starting a newspaper. I believe I was the first woman newspaper editor in southern Africa."

However, although women such as de Bruyn have had a few promotions in their media organizations at the time, she saw that for most of the women in journalism, the glass ceiling was firmly intact – they could not get promotions. The masculine newsroom was characterized by men who never talked about the necessity to treat women as equals. However, even some of these women interviewed didn't seem to have a politicized understanding of the ways in which women's subordination was being reproduced and that they could change the system. Most remained caught up into the myths of male superiority, and accepted their marginalization.

Selle also adds to the majority of the interviewees' sentiments that "during the 1970's and the 1980's there was no way you would get a woman as an editor unless they owned the newspaper."

Gender consciousness in the newsrooms

There are those women journalists interviewed who had in their own little ways some degree of gender consciousness that they incorporated into their work as reporters. They tried to use their vantage points on the inside of newsrooms to try to get women's experiences and gender analyses into the news. However, overall, this gender consciousness was not as dynamic in Namibian newsrooms at the time. Therefore, some interviewees seemed to think, retrospectively, that a lack of a vibrant gender consciousness was definitely a constraint. However, most stressed that at that time, their focus was really on the larger struggle that aimed to free that country from apartheid, and thus, women's issues were set aside for the larger course – to dismantling the apartheid system. Lister, for instance, stressed that:

> We were fighting an armed struggle and for the rights of a people who had been denied them under colonialism and apartheid. Of course, women's issues were part of this, but not the exclusive focus at the time.

However, Lister's then colleague at *The Namibian*, Sue Cullinan, added that "I don't think we consciously brought a women's perspective into the news (Lister's column was called 'political perspective' after all), but perhaps we saw things from a more humanistic point of view."

Similarly, de Bruyn points out that "Gender was never an issue at that time. We never had a gender agenda… the first time that I became aware of gender issues and that it was important, it was after independence and that was with very strong women returning from exile, like Pendukeni, and like Ndaitwah, and Libertine." These women, whom de Bruyn mentioned later became the first women government ministers in independent Namibia.

However, despite lack of an explicit gender agenda in the apartheid era newsrooms, there were a few open women media activists such as Erastus, introduced earlier in this chapter, who fought her way to get her editor's approval of her column on women issues at the *Times of Namibia* newspaper, where she made her *debut* into the field of journalism just before Namibia's independence in 1990. Erastus's former editor, Carol Kotze, recalls that when Erastus asked if she could write such a column, they let her do so anyway since that's what she wanted to do. Erastus recalls: "I used to write a column mainly for women that was every Wednesday and basically I just used to cover more of women and children issues. Of course, I could also do some other stories but my task was more to cover women, children and social oriented issues." Erastus added that:

> I had to actually fight for the column because a lot of women issues were coming up especially in Namibia. Issues of gender were coming up, issues of representation of women in different institutions. That column made me a bit famous because that was the only newspaper with a column focusing on women issues by then. What I used to do normally, I would cover different kinds of issues but I would always have a profile of these emerging women either as a parliamentarian or a woman in a financial institution, not only prominent women but I was also looking at students and grassroots women, just depending on what was emerging at that particular time and I would make it an issue.

Erastus added that women's issues in other media outlets were really not much considered despite that a lot of women organizations were coming just towards independence and trying to sensitize women, but the coverage was very minimum.

Women journalists as mothers

Women journalists who were also mothers faced another kind of gender constraints, claiming that there was no support for them during maternity leave. According to Cullinan, "the more difficult issue was juggling work and home, trying to raise children at the same time as hold down a full-time (and over-time!)". Cullinan's sentiments were echoed by Lucy who said that: "I also don't think there was any support for female journalists who were also mothers. Many had to quietly juggle their maternal roles and responsibilities with their journalistic careers."

Although Kotze mentioned in the interview that she did not feel treated differently while executing her journalism duties in the industry as a woman, she said at one time she had to take leave from her job as a journalist and took up a job as a school teacher, a profession she found to have more flexible working hours. In her own words, Kotze said: "In 1976, I stopped working as a journalist because by then I had three children and couldn't continue running around to cover news… after other jobs such as teaching and lecturing, I went back to journalism in 1990 as editor at the *Times of Namibia*." She went back to journalism when her children grew a bit older.

Meanwhile, Honey thinks there were very few women journalists in Namibia because the nature of the job held many women back those days. Honey said:

> A lot of women had kids and they were married and their husbands could not let them go all over the country at the funny hours and so, I don't think they were particularly gender held but it was just sort of an inconvenient sector, so they took jobs with fix hours such as subbing, they didn't go out there covering stories as much. But I think there were quite a few of them doing the fix-hour jobs. That's my impression anyway.

This statement by Honey also illustrates the institutionalized patriarchal control that husbands were privileged to have over the Namibian women, including some of the female journalists interviewed for the study. And this by extension indirectly also restricted the types of assignments they were sometimes able to explore compared to their male colleagues.

In sum, this chapter has highlighted some of the gender-related constraints that these women journalists had to endure both at the macro-level of the Namibian society during the apartheid era, as well as at the micro-level as demonstrated by their various experiences in the newsroom.

8 Women Journalists and Intimidation: Political Constraints

This chapter delves further into a discussion about what women journalists have reported regarding the political obstacles that were placed upon them, all of which they had to struggle against just to do their jobs as journalists.

Government intimidation and death threats

Journalists, particularly those who worked for *The Namibian*, were regarded as threats to the ruling regime. As mentioned earlier in this study, *The Namibian* newspaper was regarded as a SWAPO party mouthpiece at the time. According to Lister, there were campaigns against her – jailing, harassment, intimidation, death threats, assassination plots, smear pamphlets, etc. These campaigns showed that the then authorities thought women could be 'dealt with' and neutralized more easily than men in the struggle. Lister further says:

> Not only did I have to work in circumstances and length of time that most people could not, would not work today, but my family tried to persuade me to do something else, fearing risks to my life. My partners also felt the heat from my political convictions, and later on, my children also paid a price, by seeing their mother arrested, detained, tried, etc. I was also in detention without trial while a few months pregnant with my daughter.

While *The Namibian* newspaper is much freer now to use reporters' names on the 'bylines', the most common 'byline' on, particularly, political articles in *The Namibian* during the apartheid system was, for instance, 'Staff Reporter'. Damases recalled that it was very common for the newspaper to use the generic 'Staff Reporter' byline in order to protect the identity of the reporter if the article was on a sensitive issue to avoid the harassments by the apartheid regime that she claims were pervasive at the time. However, according to Damases, sometimes the editor, Lister, would put her own name because she "knew the entire pros and cons." Damases also said that, while today, in independent Namibia, reporters in Namibia have freedom of movement, in those days, she says, one had to watch their back. "Like in town, you would not just go there and socialize like now during independence, and speaking your mind… during those days you were always scared that they could be hunting for you for the story that you wrote."

Government 'black' list

Reporters who dared to challenge the regime were often barred from covering certain government activities. For instance, Lister used to travel to the northern war zone with the former South African Defense Force (SADF) in military vehicles and planes to cover war activities, but SADF later put her on their 'blacklist' and refused her accreditation because she was perceived a SWAPO supporter. Similarly, Selle, who also occasionally covered some military-related stories, says that she at one point sort of became *persona non grata* with the military, and was prevented from getting their "favored scoops" because they suspected she was anti-apartheid.

Damases adds that:

> You know, basically during the apartheid system you would go to the war zone [for news coverage] and at one time, we were flown to the war zone by the military and wrote a story on the PLAN fighters who were tied to the Caspers [big armored vehicles] and we took some pictures. But whatever we wanted to cover was monitored by the system. So, if you wrote something that did not go according to what they dictated to you, that's why you would always write a story and put 'staff reporter'. We went to cover an aftermath of a battle field between SADF and PLAN combatants.

Damases adds that another issue was:

> When the system [apartheid regime] did not want to take male journalists [with it to cover events at the battle field] then they also took the women because they felt it was easier to dictate to women. But, us women, what we did, we still came back and reported objectively and using the famous "staff reporter" as a byline. But, of course, the system would always find out [the author of that particular news story].

In other words, despite the uniform discriminatory nature of the apartheid system across gender of the Namibian black community (men and women), however, there were occasions when women suffered more because they were considered as 'softer targets'. Therefore, what Damases is saying in the above statement simply demonstrates one such example, but in this case orchestrated against women journalists. What's interesting, however, is that regardless of what clearly appeared to be a selective of putting these women in harm's way (being sent to cover stories in the battle field), they still courageously maintained their commitment to the journalistic ethical standards in reporting those stories. In summary, therefore, this chapter had shed some light in bringing to the fore some of the political constraints these women journalists faced during the liberation struggle of Namibia. However, these women also suffered some race-related constraints, the nature of which will be explained in the following chapter.

9 Black Women Journalists and Racial Constraints

The lack of support for black women journalists

Both black and white women interviewees acknowledged that black journalists perhaps felt the pinch of racial constraints in executing their journalism duties more than their white counterparts. According to Gwen Lister, at the height of the struggle, apart from the black Namibian women they (at *The Namibian*) later trained, there were black journalists only on 'softer' beats, at the radio and later television. "They did not cover politics however." Honey, who is also white, said that while apartheid kept people out of a lot of things, she believes it did affect black women and black people in general more. She recalls that when she went to work in the 1970s and in 1985 there weren't many black women in the profession. However, she believes that black women were certainly doing the best they could under the circumstances. Coetzee, who is also a white female journalist, stressed that "it was a thousand times more difficult for black women," while the anonymous interviewee, Lucy, says:

> I would be stupid and naïve to believe that my racial classification didn't affect my prism approach to life and journalism. Even though I was an English-speaking Catholic, born to 'second class' South Africans of Greek and Portuguese origin and grew up in a conservative Afrikaans town outside Johannesburg, I still had a lot more opportunities than the majority of 'black' South Africans (and Namibians).

De Bruyn, who as mentioned earlier in this study worked for the national broadcasting corporation, SWABC, during the apartheid regime and now works as one of the senior journalists at *Die Republikein* newspaper, also believes that the apartheid system had a great impact upon black women. In this regard, de Bruyn points out: "I was not affected but for instance, I think it's only been about three years ago that we had the first black female colleague here [at *Die Republikein*]". She also did not recall seeing any applications for journalism positions by black women when she worked for the national broadcasting corporation before independence. She says: "I can't think of going out on a story with a black female reporter, it's weird… but now things have changed… because if I now look at for instance NAMPA and *New Era* (these are government media parastatals), there are incredible competent journalists that are black women."

According to black woman journalist Theodora Nandjaa, the field of journalism during that time was perceived as a preserve for whites. Due to the Bantu educational system, the black population in Namibia was almost confirmed to two professions – teaching and nursing. Erastus adds that:

> As you know the situation in Namibia then (as a black person) you were only supposed to be either a teacher or a nurse…. I was the only black woman [in her newsroom at the *Times of Namibia*] and the majority of the other women who were there were white women, and there wasn't much of a relationship between me and them that we could really say what was happening, but we could make jokes about the men… they [white women] were even in a better position than me as a black woman because they were editors and I was just a mere journalist.

Meanwhile, one of the apartheid laws that was enacted by the Nationalist Party government in South Africa was the Bantu Education Act of 1953. This Act codified several aspects of the apartheid system, and its major provision enforced separation of races in all educational institutions. Furthermore, universities were made 'tribal' and many mission schools had to be closed. The National Party's rationale was that the blacks had a different culture, separate from that of the whites, and that they had to be educated accordingly. The Party argued that black schools should meet the requirements of the Bantu community and not of an integrated South African European Community (Ndilula, 1988). Ndilula (1988) further explains that the Bantu education was designed in a way that the 'Bantu people' (black people) are only given enough education to serve their communities but not good enough to compete with the European community in South Africa and by extension, in Namibia. For example, no science or mathematics was taught under Bantu education; emphasis was placed on agriculture since the system wanted black people to be uneducated farmers, not scientists or mathematicians. And as Nandjaa and Erastus stated above, indeed the Bantu educational system confined black people to teaching and nursing and they practiced the two professions in their own black community. These were almost the highest prestigious professions the majority of black people could venture into, and hence very few blacks in professions such as journalism.

Mwase (1988) posits that in both television and radio, there was no training of indigenous Namibians by colonial authorities in the field of journalism worth mentioning. Most skilled mass media positions were staffed by white Namibians and South African personnel. But on the other hand, those Namibians in exile, through efforts by SWAPO and the United Nations Institute for Namibia, received some training conducted particularly in Zambia under the Namibia Nationhood Program, focusing, for example, on training of technicians (studio operators, transmitters, announcers) in radio program production and equipment maintenance.

Similarly, the Bantu educational system has been blamed for causing unsuccessful stories among the history of black people during the apartheid era. Authors such as Unterhalter (1988) have blamed the Bantu educational system on the 'pitifully small' literature on Namibia because black people could not be educated enough to conduct their own empirical studies to document their history accordingly. This largely contributed to the invisibility of women, because in the event that a scholar wrote something on Namibia during the apartheid era, it would be on institutions in which women played no role, and aspects of economic production where women's work is not observed (Unterhalter, 1988).

Therefore, according to Erastus, as a black woman journalist, it almost felt as though it was a privilege for her to become a journalist. Erastus further argued that one remained confined in that environment and sometimes failed to even notice various constraints because the journalists were made to feel that they were being given a favor just by being permitted entry into white (and male dominated) environment.

Damases, the first black woman journalist to be hired at *The Namibian* in 1988, also experienced some racial constraints, particularly because she was a black woman in a male-dominated field. She stressed that the system did not respect women in general, let alone a black one. Therefore, she emphasized that as a black woman journalist, her race affected her immensely. She said that because of this pervasive racism and sexism, she didn't feel supported by her supervisor. She said:

> If I had the support from those I was working with, today I could have been one of the top journalists today [in the country]. I have inspired a lot of journalists like yourself [pointing at the researcher] and the list is long. So, if I also had people who inspired me I was probably going to be one of the top journalists of this country, but I didn't have that support system. And if I was a black male journalist, I could have been in a better position because a lot of black male journalists still continue, but all black women journalists that worked as reporters during the liberation struggle are no longer practicing.

Damases added that Erastus is now in the fishery profession, and although Theodora Nandjaa is still in the media industry, she has left the newsroom and is now performing public relations and marketing work at the NBC. Damases herself left *The Namibian* newspaper and took up a job as a court translator and later moved on to other professions. Damases further said that her news organization (*The Namibian*) used to have journalists from abroad who would come to work with them for a period of time, even for as long as six months at a time, and they always tipped them (staff at *The Namibian* including the editor) that *The Namibian* newspaper could get funding from the international community for further training in journalism abroad. "So, I remember making that request to *The Namibian* but nobody considered it. So you end up getting frustrated and if you get a better job offer elsewhere then you just leave. And that's what happened in my case.

I quit and I went to translate at the court because of my bi-lingual skills." Damases is actually multi-lingual.

Meanwhile, Damases still dreams of returning to the field. She added that she hopes to have a column on women's issues in one of the local newspapers. Erastus, who said she joined journalism because she wanted to be a writer and used journalism as a gateway to achieve her dream, also still believes that one day she will establish herself as a writer.

Black woman journalist Nandjaa believed that, for a woman, particularly a black woman to survive all the constraints that women journalists faced at the time, a black female journalist had to be strong and quite extraordinary. You could hardly make it if you were just your ordinary woman in the street, she said. Damases is known for her firm and strong character, and as mentioned earlier, a lot of black women who joined the field after independence were in one way or another inspired by Damases, including this researcher.

Black women suffered the most of all kinds of discrimination, for first and foremost of being black, then a woman. One of the women who followed the second path cited in Byerly and Ross's (2006) study suggests, for instance, that black women journalists had to fight much harder than white women to gain advancement in South Africa. Their white counterparts have had the historical advantage of a better education and social position, which sometimes makes it hard for them to empathize with the experiences of black women.

In her interview with this researcher, Kotze argued that women, particularly white women, had a chance to get educated if they had wanted to during the liberation, and in independent Namibia. And this opportunity was extended to black women as well. However, according to Kotze, women did not seem to have utilized the opportunity effectively. As such, "That is why I said (earlier) they sometimes make their own inequality to a certain extent because they don't grab the chance," she added.

'Sell outs'

However, it is important to point out that black female journalists were not the only ones who experienced race constraints. Although Lister said she is not sure if her race, as a white person, helped or hindered her ability to perform her work as a journalist, she remarked that, "I was an anathema to the authorities: A 'white' woman who had 'sold out' to what they perceived as the communist movement, SWAPO. So this certainly put me in the firing line." Lister said she had one of the toughest assignments of politics and war.

And because she had entered journalism to fight apartheid and all its ramifications, she started political reporting, and covering mass SWAPO rallies. She said:

> In the latter case, I was certainly the only 'white' person present, apart from security police who sat in their cars at a distance watching the proceedings and monitoring the people who were present. Often these rallies were violently broken up and I was targeted by the police. But this put me in immediate touch with the people and enabled my political reporting as Namibians learned to trust me and give me information.

Kotze, who worked for pro-government newspapers at the time such as *The Republikein* and the *Times of Namibia,* claims that she was also accused very regularly by her own colleagues of "being left, and a communist and liberal and a 'Kaffir Boetie'[1] because I was the only one with black friends sitting down like with you (motioning to the way she was sitting down together in a café like old friends with this black researcher during this interview. So my colleagues looked at me with great suspicion," Kotze added.

---

[1] Apartheid-era South African term of abuse for "white people friendly with indigenous Africans.

10 Resistance and Complicity

How did women journalists deal with the gender, political and racial constraints during that era? In exploring this Research Question Two, two categories emerged from the answers provided by the women journalists interviewed for the study. These categories were (1) resistance and (2) acceptance, both of which will be discussed in greater detail in the following section.

Resistance

The effort by the women journalists interviewed for this study to resist gender-related newsroom politics was exemplified in the ways with which they rejected any attempt to confine them to softer assignments, by resorting to setting up their own newspapers, and demanding the right to be treated as equals to their male counterparts.

With regard to their resistance against accepting inferior assignments, some of the women journalists interviewed for the study described some specific responses to this type of challenge. For example, Lucy and de Bruyn went out of their way to demand that they be assigned to cover political and military assignments – the type of stories that were usually the special preserve of male journalists. While in the case of Lister, she started her own media outlet, *The Namibian*, and Coetzee and Rogge started *Sister Namibia*. According to Coetzee, due to a lack of a strong women's perspective in those years, definitely not from a libertarian or feminist perspective, she says, this partly influenced her and other women such as Rogge to form the women's publication. Coetzee added:

> Women in the apartheid regime I personally saw two options. One was to be co-opted by the regime, another was to be subversive in a cultural way – to become untouchable by removing oneself from the predominant culture, which was male, racist and heterosexual. This was the option I chose.

Taken as a whole, these two courageous stands by these women to reject stereotypes could also serve as an illustration of their conscious demand to be treated as nothing less than their male colleagues.

Acceptance

Although some of the interviewees showed a clear resistance in dealing with political constraints as indicated above, others followed a different approach including complicity in their own oppression. Therefore, this part of the discussion is an attempt to show how complicity was adopted by some of the women interviewed as they faced political constraints in the newsroom.

According to Byerly and Ross (2006), women's complicity may be best understood within the framework of masculine hegemony. Italian intellectual Antonio Gramsci's concept of hegemony has come to be understood to mean non-coercive ways by which the dominant class obtains the consent of the less powerful.

Although some of the women interviewed, such as Lister, Selle, and Lucy, fought through their way in the patriarchal (and apartheid) media environment, some did not dare to fight the constraints they faced as women journalists. According to Sarah Damases, she just had to go with the flow, arguing that if you complained too much, you would find yourself jobless. She said this was clearly a constraint. Therefore, it can be argued that it is clear that women did not always have guts to speak out against these sort of discrimination they saw, and many still found it easier to go along with rules of a male-dominated work place because it was easier than embarking on a constant fight against a patriarchal system when there was a more grave issue to fight – the dismantling of apartheid.

One of the women interviewees, Lötter, added that some women had to accept the fact that women are supposed to be submissive to their male counterparts. For instance, she said that women in her newsroom were expected to dress and behave in a certain way and they did.

11 Reporting Injustices, Fighting Gender Inequality

What do women journalists identify as their journalistic contributions to the liberation struggle of the country? This Research Question Three sought answers to what their work and effort meant to the struggle and/or to women. As a result, two categories were found to be most representative of their responses: (1) racial equality and justice, and (2) gender equality.

However, in discussing this question, a distinction has to be made between the women journalists who consciously and actively participated in the national liberation struggle, and those who were indirectly drawn into the struggle by virtue of being journalists during this period. Among those that fall into the first category were such as: Lister, Damases, Nandjaa, and Cullinan. The special characteristic of these women journalists was that they worked for anti-apartheid media, or later on, left a state media to form their own independently. These women may be said to have contributed directly to the struggle for independence through their work.

On the other hand, the second category were women journalists like Kotze, Erastus, de Bruyn, Lötter, Lucy, Selle, Rogge, Coetzee, and Honey who worked for media institutions sympathetic to the status quos. In the interview with these women, some of them such as Kotze, Lötter, de Bruyn pointed out that they did not contribute directly to the liberation struggle. Others such as Lucy did in their own little ways. These differences will be fully explained in the sections that follow.

Reporting injustices and atrocities

Testimonies from some of these participants clearly indicate that women journalists played a significant role during the liberation struggle. Some of these women journalists believe they played significant roles in the liberation struggle in various ways. However, about half of the interviewees pointed to Gwen Lister as the principal woman journalist who was in the forefront in exposing atrocities against the Namibian people by the apartheid regime. Lister said she entered journalism to fight apartheid:

> I certainly did make inroads on the South African propaganda machine by trying to show the 'human' face of SWAPO. I was also probably the only white person to do so, apart from a handful of white males who supported SWAPO, mainly lawyers etc. I, along with my colleagues, also exposed the atrocities of the SA [South Africa] regime against the people of Namibia, primarily those supporting SWAPO, and served to bring international attention

to their plight. We were fighting an armed struggle and for the rights of a people who had been denied them under colonialism and apartheid.

According to Honey, "My editor Gwen Lister, for instance, is one person who played a huge role, and continues to play a big role. She happened to be there and she used her position to do all sort of things." Another interviewee, Erastus said:

> I only became a journalist just before independence and during that period, I really tried to bring out issues concerning women… but there are women like Gwen Lister, we all know her… she really played a major role. She's been jailed and so forth.

Similarly, Rogge also acknowledged that there were a few individual women journalists who played a significant role, such as:

> Gwen Lister obviously, Jean Sutherland who flip-flopped from here to there but also had her role to play … people like Rianne Selle, even if she worked in the background but was always within government structures as such she made the transition from the old regime… a lot of people [women journalists] came through under Rianne's management. Rianne has been involved across the transition period from a media management point of view," Rogge said.

Cullinan believes that they, as women journalists, played a role in leading by example. "The fact that we were determined to work in news, even with other responsibilities, showed that we were not only as good as anyone else (and better!) but that we could multi-task. It also showed that that politics was important to us and we needed to be involved at every level."

These interviewees' testimonies indicate various ways in which women journalists made their own contributions, both large and small, to the liberation struggles. For instance, Nandjaa, who worked as a budding journalist at the Namibian Council of Churches' newsletter, said because she was a woman, she was sometimes sent on undercover missions to cover issues the system would not want the public to know about. For instance, at one time, she said, because she was a woman, she was sent to go with some women who were going to petition to the headmen of some village in Northern Namibia, protesting against an army base of the apartheid regime that was set-up near a school. These women petitioners argued that their children were potentially in danger should the SWAPO fighters decide to attack the army base. They argued that, although they believed that SWAPO fighters would not intentionally want to harm the children, these school kids could be caught up in the cross-fire. So this was a good opportunity for Nandjaa to join in as one of the petitioners and brought back a scoop to her newsroom, subsequently exposing some of these dynamics of the war. However, while Nandjaa acknowledges her little contribution to the struggle, albeit young, in her early 20s at the time, she also echoes other interviews sentiments that women such as Gwen Lister were really the real deal – they are the ones that have really played a role of informing the world out there about the brutalities of the South African forces in Namibia, Nandjaa said.

Others, such as de Bruyn, have also contributed to the liberation struggle in other ways. For example, de Bruyn believes she played a reconciliatory role. When Namibians in exile were being repatriated back to the country as part of the United Nations Resolution 435, a plan that brought about negotiations leading to Namibia's independence, there were a lot of fears among people in the white community who were mostly the beneficiaries of the apartheid regime. De Bruyn, who is a white journalist, said:

> We had to alleviate the fears of the white people in the country who were saying, 'oh gee' all these bad guys coming from exile they are going to take over the country … we had to explain the role of democracy, to bring peace, to tell people that you know what, no matter who wins this election the sun will rise tomorrow … you will stay in the house … your kids will go to school, there is nothing to panic about … if you are a democrat you will also accept the results of the elections, if you lose. I think, perhaps in that sense, I might have played a small role.

Lucy had this to say about their contribution:

> I believe and hope I played a significant role in the creation of Namibia as a democratic country. It was exciting to witness, document, report on and be part of the transformation and change. My Namibian experience was definitely an excellent training ground and precursor for my role in the transformation of South Africa and the South African Broadcasting Corporation, SABC.

Lötter believes that she probably played a small role by using her position in the broadcasting corporation as a reporter to tone down the pro-government propaganda that the state machine (SWABC) exerted to advance and maintain the status quo. Selle adds that you couldn't really find women journalists who could have played a significant role in the liberation struggle at mainstream media such as that played by journalists at *The Namibian* newspaper. She said:

> I think if it wasn't for Gwen Lister, Jean Sutherland and all those other leaders there, we would not have seen the reports of what was really happening in this country in the North (dubbed the war zone at the time). They were the first to report the atrocities. When the military would just flatten a homestead when they suspected that there were SWAPO soldiers there … I think *The Namibian* played a major role. In the government service, we had a policy that we would not write about the military.

Fighting gender inequality

Women have also contributed in varying ways to gender equality, although not always in an explicit way. For instance, Erastus' column tried to bring out issues concerning women. However, her paper, the *Times of Namibia*, was the only one with a column focusing on women issues by then. Other women journalists such as Lucy also contributed in her own way. She said:

> I find that I subconsciously seek out women interviewees because they're natural storytellers, who don't often hide their emotions. My ears also prick up when I only hear a handful of women's voices and views in the news. The unofficial initiatives that I've taken are to mentor and encourage young female journalists.

Rogge, who was one of the founding members of *Sister Namibia* along side women such as Coetzee in 1989, said perhaps their contribution to the liberation struggle was the establishment of *Sister Magazine*. The fact that there were no publications looking specifically at women's issues motivated them to start the magazine. "*Sister* tried to bring that consciousness to women and to participate in the (forthcoming) new democracy and so on and so forth," said Rogge. Coetzee adds that: "We realized that Namibia was moving towards political liberation and the founders (of *Sister*) wanted to participate in finding new roles for women."

However, Rogge noted that although individual women journalists played their own little roles during the liberation struggle inside Namibia, she feels the larger role was really played by those Namibian women who were in exile. She had an impression that those exiled women would have had more consciousness about the roles that they could play because they were actively involved in the struggle, but for those who remained behind (in Namibia), society and life just went on as normal and they didn't question the status quo as far as women's positions in the society were concerned. This is a clear indication that patriarchal hegemony was rife during apartheid Namibia.

Selle also argued that Namibian women in exile developed a feminist consciousness first, because of their participation in international women's conferences. On the other hand, Namibians inside the country could not have those opportunities given that the apartheid regime had kept Namibia in seclusion and hence depriving its citizens to take part in international undertakings or activism. Selle added that Namibian women in exile had an opportunity to share ideas with other international women at conferences such as the United Nations one held in Nairobi, Kenya in 1985. According to Byerly and Ross (2006), the United Nations has since the establishment of the United Nations Commission on the Status of Women in 1964, been proving to be an international space for women's rights to be advanced. It can be argued that these forums are an opportunity for women working in a range of independent organizations around the world to hold open exchanges with each other in order to identify distinct problems within nations, but also commonalities and shared visions around issues (Byerly and Ross, 2006).

In conclusion, as mentioned earlier, although few of these women journalists interviewed for this study did seem to distance themselves from the usage of the word "feminism", it can be argued that they did gain some feminist political consciousness as they began to view their profession as an opportunity to advance women's view and status, apart from the larger struggle – which was to liberate Namibia from the yolk of colonialism under an apartheid regime. In addition, they can be said to have served in a feminist capacity by creating precedents and role models for other women in the field later.

12 Conclusion

This study adds to our understanding of what we know about the role of women journalists in Namibia's liberation struggle. The foregoing pages have described the critical role played by many women journalists during the liberation struggle of Namibia. The narratives of the women have also highlighted the many constraints that women journalists have been forced to endure in the male-dominated newsrooms in Namibia, as well as the ways they coped and transcended those constraints.

In this study, first chapters introduced the background, significance, the statement of the problem and presented the feminist media theoretical framework as one of the many loosely related theories in the Marxist critical tradition. Following chapters examined the related literature and discussed the methodology used in conducting this qualitative research study. The final chapters reported the findings and analyzed them according to the research questions of the present study. This conclusion discusses the theoretical implication of the findings, the study's limitations, and directions for future research.

As the literature reviewed in Chapter one indicates, few scholars have studied the role of the media in national liberation struggles. Even more glaring is the absence of studies on the role of women journalists during national liberation struggles such as that in Namibia. Therefore, it was of critical importance to study the roles played by Namibian women journalists, and the constraints they endured, and their coping mechanisms so that one could successfully contribute to the body of scholarship on Namibian history, women and media, the feminist movement and other intellectual stake holders that could benefit from the study, including policy makers.

This study sought to answer three research questions:

1. What gender and race-related constraints, if any, did Namibian women journalists confront in their news organizations during the liberation years?
2. How did women journalists deal with these constraints during that era?
3. What do they identify as their journalistic contributions to the liberation struggle of the country?

The findings as they relate to the above research questions indeed indicate that although Namibian women journalists made significant contributions to the liberation struggle, they were also forced to operate in an environment fraught with various constraints – political, gender and race. With regards to the first research question, the majority of the women journalists interviewed said that inequality in the Namibian media industry was quite blatant. The power dynamics of working in this field caused women to feel discriminated against by their male colleagues, who invariably held positions of power and authority. They were not hired in decision-making positions, were given less valued assignments, and were required to work quite diligently to merely be considered for more challenging assignments such as political beats, military and economic matters, and issues that fell in the category "of hard news." Indeed these matters were almost always reserved for their male journalist counterparts.

With regards to the second question, while a few women decided to comply with the status quo, a few such as Gwen Lister, Jo Rogge and Estelle Coetzee left the male-dominated media institutions and went to establish their own publications. Lister's newspaper, *The Namibian,* has since its founding in 1985 been the country's leading independent media outlet under the leadership of Lister. Rogge and Coetzee co-founded *Sister Namibia,* which since its founding in 1989, continues to be the leading feminist publication in the country. Other women journalists interviewed such as Lucy, Estelle de Bruyn, Anna Erastus, Rianne Selle worked harder in their day-to-day profession to overcome these constraints.

The findings related to the last research question of the study indicate that most of the women felt that they made their own small contributions in one way or another, but most of them pointed their fingers to Lister who was considered to have played an unprecedented role as far as exposing brutalities that were inflicted upon the indigenous Namibian people by the apartheid regime.

On the other hand, there does exist a body of research that speaks to the idea that during society-wide liberation struggles, women tend not to focus on woman's issues until the broader freedoms are achieved. From this study, it's clear that women journalists saw their political freedom as the first and foremost priority before their freedom as women. This, too, in and of itself might be categorized by the feminist approach as normalizing male issues and incorporating them in their professions (Byerly and Ross, 2006).

Theoretical implications

In the vein of feminist critical theory of the media, it is clear that women journalists had a significant role to contribute to the liberation struggle, but this role was fraught with many obstacles due to not only the apartheid environment under which they had to operate but also because due to the patriarchal and hegemonic system in which they were immersed. Some women got co-opted into the "macho" newsroom, which was always fraught with patriarchal attitudes that assume women's inferiority to men.

In their book *Women and the Media: A Critical Introduction,* Byerly and Ross (2006) have put forth the idea of "unmasking the 'macho' newsroom" which is generally defined by scholars as the "incorporation of women journalists into a traditionally male profession has the effect of 'normalizing' what are essentially male-identified concern and a male-directed agenda" (p. 78–9). There are four major characteristics associated with this framework: 1) discriminatory allocation of news stories, 2) gender-blindness, 3) incorporation, and 4) retreat.

Incorporation, for instance, is defined as a response that "requires women to take on so-called masculine styles, values, and reporting behaviors such as "objectivity". It can therefore be argued that women journalists such as Carol Kotze and Carmen Honey fit into this category because, unlike most of the women interviewed who thought gender discrimination was very blatant during the liberation, the two said they did not really feel discriminated against because they were women journalists, except on one or two occasions during their careers as journalists during the liberation struggle.

Another issue, the concept of "unmasking the 'Macho' newsroom" put forward is the *discriminatory allocation of news stories,* defined as the "pigeonholing of women journalists into narrow topics typically thought of as "women's issues" (Byerly and Ross, 2006, p. 80). Women in this study have indicated that discrimination of allocation of news is one of the grave constraints they had to face in their careers as journalists at that time. In fact, this practice of assigning "soft news" to women has long been condemned by feminist scholars all over the world. It's an issue that has often created tension between male journalists and their female counterparts. Women interviewed in this study, such as Lucy, had to fight her way and made it clear to her supervisors that she was not interested in covering the "First lady's tea parties" and other news events that were considered trivial .

Another concept this framework posits is the issue of gender-blindness, which is defined as a situation in which women use "the convenient example of their own success as a means by which to refute the suggestion of sexism in the industry" (Byerly and Ross, 2006, p. 80). Although there was not a vibrant gender consciousness in the newsrooms in Namibia during the liberation struggle because of their number one pre-occupation of dismantling apartheid, these women were not gender blind except for a few such as Carol Kotze, who argued that sometimes women were to blame for their own gender inequality for taking up behaviors that are typically female, such as accepting the concept of male superiority. Such complicity was also raised by numerous participants in Byerly and Ross's (2006) cross-cultural research, and in Louise North's (2006) research with journalists in Tasmania, Australia.

Another concept that was worth reviewing and was found to be useful for the purpose of interpreting the findings of this present study is the concept of feminism. As mentioned in the preceding pages, Namibian women, just like many others in Africa as a whole (Mohanty, 1991), tend to distance themselves from the term "feminist." However, many of these individuals, including Anna Erastus, performed some feminist media activism work while as journalists during the study period. Under the 'unmasking of the "macho" newsroom definition, *feminist* is defined as a case "whereby journalists make a conscious decision to provide an alternative voice – for example writing on health in order to expose child abuse than continue to fight battles in the work place" (Byerly and Ross, 2006, p. 80). Therefore, it can be argued that a few of these women, such as Erastus, who had a women's issue column in her newspaper; Lucy, who consciously endeavored to include women in a news gathering and reports during her days as a reporter at South West African Broadcasting Corporation (SWABC); and Rogge and Coetzee who took an initiative to establish a feminist publication, would arguably fall under the label "feminist."

Another concept under this framework was *retreat*, defined as a situation in which "many women media workers see their decision to quit as assertive and empowering" (Byerly and Ross, 2006, p. 80). It can be argued that the decision by women such as Sarah Damases and Rianne Selle's to leave the reporting industry to venture into other sectors fits into this category.

In a nutshell, the findings of this study have therefore illustrated that generally, Namibian women journalists during the liberation struggle of the country followed some elements of Byerly and Ross's (2006) Model of Women's Media Action (MWMA), These authors developed this model following their cross-cultural examination of the ways in which women have worked inside and outside the mainstream media industries since the 1970s. In analyzing the interviews and written answers of 90 participants from 20 nations, these authors found that women's media activism can be organized into four main paths or approaches. They call the first path "politics to media"; second, "media profession to politics"; third, "advocate change agent" and the fourth path is "women's media enterprises".

According to the authors, women's media activism as "any organized effort on women's part to make changes in established media enterprises or to create new structures with the goal of expanding women's voice in society and enabling their social advancement" (p.101). This, they added, might include an increase in the number of women employed and promoted; making media content more representative of women's diverse experiences; eliminating of media stereotypes of women; changing public policy governing media operations; increasing the amount and quality of news coverage or other media about women; establishing women-owned or controlled media; and organizing women as well as men to take some kind of action relating to these media activism stipulations.

As mentioned earlier, although most of the women journalists who were interviewed for this present study did not perceive their work as journalists during the Namibian liberation struggle as that of women's media activism, the MWMA does help us to argue that most of the Namibian women journalists actually did perform some duties concurrent with the functions of what warrants one to be called a woman media activist. In analyzing their responses to interviews for this present study, it was clear that the Namibian women journalists at least followed the second and fourth paths of the Model of Media Activism (MWMA).

Also of particular interest to this study is the fact that the MWMA has an underlying concern with power relations, structures that produce them, and social change (i.e., emancipation) that places it with the critical theoretical paradigm (Byerly and Ross, 2006) which consequently broadly informs this present study, theoretically. These authors posit that the MWMA follows the structure of a critical theory because it "problematizes and then situates a phenomenon historically, reveals the structures of power (in this case, in gendered social relations) inherent in the phenomenon, and poses alternatives for change (i.e., employment of media to create a women's public sphere, etc.)" (Byerly and Ross, 2006, p.115).

Again, as mentioned earlier, women journalists such as Anna Erastus clearly followed the second path – media profession to politics – which describes the strategy followed by women employed in the media industries who decided to use their vantage point as insiders to expand women-related content (Byerly & Ross 2006, p.125). These women that follow this path are media professionals and were formally trained in a media profession.

Meanwhile, it can also be argued that others such as Gwen Lister who was forced to establish her own newspaper (*The Namibian*), and Jo Rogge and Estelle Coetzee who went to establish a feminist publication (*Sister Namibia*), also clearly followed the fourth path – a path followed by women owning their own media that gives them control over what to publish and what not to. For instance, although *Sister Namibia* was established (in 1989) just before the Namibian independence from the apartheid regime in 1990, it played a major role to sensitize women of their own rights in a bid to effect change. According to Byerly and Ross (2006), women who follow the fourth path of the Model of Media Activism had to grapple with issues like financial skills, including the location of sufficient initial capital to establish an organization and to sustain wages for their employees. This study has illustrated how women journalists such as Gwen Lister had to struggle to get donor funding to sustain her newspaper during a time when the apartheid government would have been glad if the newspaper shut done. In fact, literature on this study shows how the government extended all sorts of threats in an attempt to silence the staff at the then only newspaper that dared to challenge the status quo.

Given these women journalists' activism in the liberation struggle has also given impetus or inspiration to organizations to continue to promote and protect the interest of women in contemporary Southern Africa. For instance, women journalists associated with two advocacy groups for women in journalism, Gender Links (based in Johannesburg, South Africa), and GEMSA in Southern Africa have recently begun to organize themselves into media monitoring and training groups so as to begin to advance women within the profession. GEMSA (the Gender and Media Southern African Network), for instance, is an umbrella organization of individuals and institutions who strive to promote gender equality within and by the media (www.gemsa.org.za) GEMSA was established "to promote gender equity in the media through regional strategies that would address everything from election coverage to HIV/AIDS (Byerly and Ross, 2006).

Practical implications

One lesson might be to ensure that these issues stay on the agenda so as not to incorporate only the male perspective and so as to ensure that liberation struggles lead to the true liberation of people at all levels. Surely, liberation struggles should not be restricted in their means and their ultimate effects to men; this study should therefore serve to encourage and embolden other women living under the yoke of oppression to change their status.

As to the question of why some white women participated in the struggle against apartheid, one could argue that they were fighting it in principle. In other words, they believed that the struggle to end apartheid was an ideological one – a struggle that had to do with justice and fairness for all. Indeed, it could have been in line with their recognition of Dr. Martin Luther King's saying that "injustice anywhere is a threat to justice everywhere" (King, 1963). Furthermore, it could also have been due to their conviction that in order for them as white women to gain full equality in that society, there was a need to first help dismantle the apartheid system. There is a longer tradition to consider with regard to whites supporting black liberation. Even during the Civil Rights struggle in the United States, there were whites who were deeply involved in African American emancipation. That was also the case with the struggle in South Africa, where, for example, the famous journalist Steven Biko (and the ANC) was helped by many white South Africans in his crusade against the apartheid system. In other words, one could also argue that the struggles for the liberation of an oppressed people are replete with examples in which individuals had shown an ability to transcend their racial or gender identities in order to participate in such struggles. Therefore, this study also shows that the black liberation of Namibia was not just fought by the black population, but it was also fought by some progressive members of the white population.

With regard to the role that these women journalists have played during the liberation struggle, the findings for the study indicate that women have equally contributed to the liberation struggle. This study does not, however, claim that these women contributed to the struggle because they were women, but that their identity as women had a major impact on the role that they played or not played during the liberation. For example, even in the United States, it was well documented that a heroine such as Rosa Parks did not initially refuse to give up her seat to a white male in Montgomery, Alabama, in 1955 because she was a woman. To the contrary, this happened, first and foremost, because she was a black person tired of the treatment she and other African Americans were being subjected to by the Jim Crow laws of that era. But it was this woman's act of courage that began to turn the wheels of the Civil Rights Movement on that fateful day. Unfortunately, there have been many other women (black and white) who have played significant roles in national liberation struggles, except that these roles have not always been documented.

However, it should also be noted that women were sometimes not able to contribute to the liberation struggle in Namibia because of the various obstacles they faced as women working in a patriarchal environment. As the findings of this study have shown, inequality was blatant during that time and that women not only had to bear the brunt of the apartheid system, but they also had to deal with the oppressive patriarchal environment that favored men more than women. As a consequence, the women journalists interviewed for the study said that it took a huge toll for them to work in a male-dominated apartheid media environment. For instance, women such as Gwen Lister and Lucy explained how much they had to fight hard to get approval from the male editors and to make them recognize that they were as capable as their male colleagues.

In fact, it's not farfetched to point out that it was these types of individual efforts to break down the gender and racial barriers exhibited by these women journalists and others that ultimately inspired the struggle about gender issues in post-independent Namibia. And that it was because of these women's courage that other courageous women who came after independence were able to advance women's causes. In essence, it was these women's courage that led to the subsequent emergence of a full-blown woman's movement in Namibia – something that hardly existed before its independence. This gave rise to a situation where women media activists joined hands with other women's organizations (when needed) to tackle women's particular concerns, regardless of their political affiliations or racial identities. For instance, *Sister Namibia,* a feminist media organization is currently spearheading the campaign for 50 percent women in political office. This campaign demands that women occupy at least 50 percent of positions of power and decision-making in Namibia (Bauer, 2006). The campaign is one of the *Namibian Women's Manifesto's* seven aims which include: increasing awareness among women, men and young people of the ways in which political, social, cultural, legal and economic systems of power control girls and women; and to oppose and challenge racism, sexism, homophobia and other discourses and practices that tend to divide and oppress people. *Sister Namibia* was mandated by the Namibian women's movement to launch the manifesto in 1999 in collaboration with women and some men from women's and human rights NGOs, women in Parliament and all levels of government, political parties and individual women activists. The 50/50 campaign was later linked to a global effort sponsored by the Women's Environment and Development Organization (WEDO). The latter, based in New York, had called for the 50 percent representation of women in all areas of politics and decision-making (Bauer, 2006).

The Namibian 50 percent campaign is also actively supported by other groups in the country, including the Women's Action for Development, a grassroots-based organization that works towards the economic and political empowerment of rural women, the Namibia Girl Child Organization, which targets school girls with the goal of preparing them for future political participation, and the Namibian Media Women's Association (NAMWA), which seeks to monitor the portrayal of women and to highlight their concerns in the popular media.

It can, therefore, be argued that the involvement of *Sister Namibia* and NAMWA in the 50/50 campaign shows that women in the media are now taking their media activism at a more significant level and therefore fulfilling their social change function in society.

Recommendations for future research

It might be useful to look at the extent to which women journalists pursued feminist goals after the liberation struggle was over at a higher level or not and look into what women are doing about that. A comparative study that would involve male journalists who worked during the period of this present study to get their opinion on how they perceived the role of women journalists during the liberation struggle could also make a good study to contribute to the overall understanding of the role of the media during the liberation struggle and the gender implications. Future research could also use a quantitative approach to explore additional research questions. For example, it would be interesting to do a content analysis of the stories that women wrote, particularly those who worked in the print media. Similarly, it will be useful to content analyze the articles written by their male counterparts during the period under study, and then compare the two, in order to find out similarities or differences that may arise.

In general, most of the few studies that have investigated issues concerning women in Namibia were conducted by foreign women. It is, therefore, imperative for Namibian women, especially budding scholars, to study these issues from a domestic Namibian perspective. Even the best known Namibian scholar might lack the particular insight and experience that might be given by a native scholar, and this unique perspective could significantly improve the research to date. It would also be interesting to study these 13 women journalists' efforts in relation to GEMSA.

Limitations

Perhaps the major limitation of this study was the lack of research funds available for the researcher. This would have enabled the researcher to spend more time perusing archival materials and government documents in Namibia to hopefully uncover more of the dynamics that prevailed in the country in relation to the role of women journalists during the liberation struggle. In addition, although in the process of writing this book, this author went through microfilm copies of the newspapers to identify articles written by some women journalists during the period under study, it was not always easy to figure out who wrote what articles because a lot of them did not carry bylines. For example, Sarah Damases, one of the women journalists interviewed for the study, pointed out that in most cases only Gwen Lister was able to publish her name along with her articles in her own newspaper, *The Namibian*. This, according to Damases, could be attributed to the fact that Lister was the owner and editor of the paper. In contrasts, it was often the case that the names of other journalists (male and female) had to be protected. This was in accordance with the toxic nature of the apartheid system, in which revealing the names of journalists struggling to dismantle it would have endangered their lives.

13 Appendix

The participating journalists, their profiles, memories and assessments

This study sought to build a baseline of information about the roles and experiences of women journalists in the liberation struggle of Namibia. Therefore, the study was guided by three research questions: 1) What gender and race-related constraints, if any, did Namibian women journalists confront in their news organizations during the liberation years? 2) How did women journalists deal with these constraints during that era? 3) What do they identify as their journalistic contributions to the liberation struggle of the country?

Accordingly, the following thirteen women were interviewed by the researcher in Windhoek between July and August 2006:

1. **Gwen Lister** – Founder and editor of *The Namibian*.
2. **Sarah Damases** – Former reporter at *The Namibian*.
3. **Sue Cullinan** – Former reporter at *The Namibian*.
4. **Carol Kotze** – Former editor for the *Times of Namibia*.
5. **Anna Erastus** – Former reporter at the *Times of Namibia*.
6. **Lucy** – Former reporter at *SWABC* (pseudonym given to a participant who preferred anonymity).
7. **Rene Lötter** – Former reporter at *SWABC*.
8. **Estelle de Bruyn** – Former reporter at *SWABC*, now at *Die Republikein*.
9. **Rianne Selle** – Former reporter at a few newspapers in Namibia, and now with the Ministry of Information in Namibia.
10. **Theodora Nandjaa** – Former reporter for the *Council of Churches of Namibia (CCN) Information*.
11. **Carmen Honey** – Former reporter at a few Namibian newspapers including The Advertiser; later worked as a correspondent, from Namibia, for *South African Press Association (SAPA)*. She is now with *The Namibian*.
12. **Jo Rogge** – Co-founded *Sister Namibia*.
13. **Estelle Coetzee** – Co-founded *Sister Namibia*.

As outlined in Chapter VI this researcher, making use of semi-structured interviews with the participants, sought answers to a range of questions such as:

- the kind of assignments they got from their editors (i.e., the kind of stories they wrote and whether they got those stories to cover based on the fact that they were women or whether they were allowed to report on tough assignments such as war);
- what efforts these Namibian women journalists made to cover women and women's issues in their stories and what criteria they used;
- whether Namibian women journalists believe they brought a "women's perspective" into their news;
- what influenced their gender-consciousness if they were;
- whether Namibian women journalists formally connected to a feminist-oriented movement now(i.e., belonging to a professional or civic organization catering for the interest of women;
- how blatant, if any, gender inequality was in Namibia's media institutions during the struggle, and if they could give their personal experience, if any;
- how the apartheid system impacted on gender equality in Namibia in general and on women journalists in particular, and whether it was based on any legal framework or whether it was a result of cultural orientation or both;
- whether or not they felt their race affected their ability to perform their work as journalists;
- whether there encountered specific obstacles as women journalists in their attempt to get to decision-making responsibilities in media organizations;
- whether they took any initiative/s to affect any kind of influence geared towards the realization of gender equality within media institutions;
- whether women journalists were represented at all at decision-making levels of the media world in Namibia;
- whether they believe they played a significant role in the liberation struggle, and if so, what do they believe that to be;
- the survival mechanisms, if any, they employed in order to survive in not only a male dominated media industry, but also in an apartheid environment;
- whether there was an organized feminist agenda in the newsrooms at the time;
- what prices, if any, women had to pay in order to work in a male-dominated apartheid media environment;
- whether they got formal journalistic training before they became journalists?;
- and whether the media institution they worked for provided them with any formal training in journalism?

The following sections provide *slightly edited extracts* from the interviewees' responses to the researcher's questions. The oral and spontaneous qualitiy of the responses has been kept. For the interview context the reader is refered to Chapter VI of this book.

Gwen Lister

- Namibian women journalists suffered gender-related constraints in the liberation years. From 1975, when I started here [in Windhoek] as a journalist, I faced immediate constraints. First of all, the fact that I wanted to become a political reporter stunned my then Editor, Hannes Smith. He believed women belonged in the kitchen! But I was insistent, and he in turn gave me a baptism of fire, the likes of which would have caused most men to flee. I started work in the early hours of the morning until late at night. I was given a huge range of tasks – undoubtedly an attempt on the part of the Editor to 'break' me and prove his point that women couldn't do the job. However, in later years, he was first to acknowledge that I was one of the best workers he had ever had. The huge range of tasks given me, although daunting, did help to prepare me with all the skills I needed to start my own newspaper years down the line.
- I had one of the toughest assignments. Politics and war. Because I had entered journalism to fight apartheid and all its ramifications, I started with political reporting, and covering mass Swapo rallies. In the latter case, I was certainly the only 'white' person present, apart from security police who sat in their cars at a distance watching the proceedings and monitoring the people who were present. Often these rallies were violently broken up and I was targeted by the police. But this put me in immediate touch with the people and enabled my political reporting as Namibians learned to trust me and give me information. In the early years I would also travel to the northern war zone, for a period also with the former South African Defense Force in military vehicles and planes. it was not long however, before the SADF put me on their 'blacklist' and refused me accreditation due to the fact that I was perceived as a Swapo supporter.
- We were fighting an armed struggle and for the rights of a people who had been denied them under colonialism and apartheid. Of course women's issues were part of this, but not the exclusive focus at the time.
- There were very few women journalists at the time who did anything more than 'soft' news.
- I am a member of the International Women's Media Foundation [IWMF] in the US. On the local front, I have worked more with Media Institute of Southern Africa [MISA] and as a founder member, actively worked for women's rights in this context. I have my reservations about women's only groups and what they can achieve without working to

change the perceptions of men at the same time. Neither were there such groups in the struggle years.

- Women were simply not considered then for 'dangerous' work. It was the almost exclusive preserve of men, except for those women like myself, who started their own media, and I don't think there were any others, apart from myself, in Namibia at the time.
- Women bore the brunt in so many ways. Not necessarily only journalists. Although the campaigns against me – jailing, harassment, intimidation, death threats, assassination plots, smear pamphlets etc – showed that the then authorities thought women could be 'dealt with' and neutralised more easily than men in the struggle.
- [I] can only speak for myself. At the height of the struggle, apart from the black Namibian women we later trained, there were black journalists only on 'softer' beats, at the radio and later television. They did not cover politics however. Not sure in my case whether race helped or hindered me. I was an anathema to the authorities. A 'white' woman who had 'sold out' to what they perceived as the communist movement, Swapo. So this certainly put me in the firing line.
- There were little or no women in decision making in media at that time. I would not have had such power if I hadn't created the position for myself by starting a newspaper. I believe I was the first woman newspaper editor in southern Africa. Women are fairly well represented in the media in Namibia now. The Namibian, for eg, is essentially a women-run newspaper, with the top positions being held by women, and near 50 per cent representation across the broad spectrum of our employees. Also woman are more likely now, to take on controversial posts in media, which was not the case before.
- I guess my role was significant. I certainly did make inroads on the South African propaganda machine by trying to show the 'human' face of Swapo, a movement they sought to prevent from coming to power at all costs. I was also probably the only white person to do so, apart from a handful of white males who supported Swapo, mainly lawyers etc. I showed that not all whites supported the status quo, although most did. I, along with my colleagues, also exposed the atrocities of the SA regime against the people of Namibia, primarily those supporting Swapo, and served to bring international attention to their plight. –
- It took a huge toll. Not only did I have to work in circumstances and length of time that most people could not, would not work today, but my family tried to persuade me to do something else, fearing risks to my life. My partners also felt the heat from my political convictions, and later on, my children also paid a price, by seeing their mother arrested, detained, tried etc. I was also in detention without trial while a few months pregnant with my daughter.

- No, I have never had formal journalistic training. Not then, not now. I have learned through baptism of fire as I mentioned earlier. Hard work and incredible commitment.

Sarah Damases
- I was born and bred in Windhoek, raised by a single parent. My mother was the one who motivated me to be what I am today. She was a house keeper. I was married and divorced now, have four children. I joined journalism in 1988 at *The Namibian* as a trainee journalist. I am a trained teacher; I was the first black woman journalist at the Namibian.
- As a woman during that time one faced a lot of gender constraints. During the liberation struggle, when it came to stories that had value, it was always assigned to male journalists. When it was just a petty issue, then it was assigned to you. But since you were just an employ, you had no rights to fight for what you thought you could make a better story out of . So what happened that time, there were assignments given... even if you were the one with the hint, the story was not given to you, it was given to somebody else... especially because the environment was male dominated. Gwen Lister is the one who assigned the stories and she gave them to the men. And that time I didn't even have a driving license so the male journalists had the privileges of driving... and I was also a trainee journalist. Hence I just had to go with the flow otherwise if you complained too much, then tomorrow you don't have a job... and one had to provide bread and butter especially for some of us who have extended families.
- During that time, it was during the transition of the liberation of Namibia. If for instance there were two political rallies going on, a male colleague would be assigned to a SWAPO rally while I, as a woman, would be assigned to a rally of a less popular political party... because then when I go there, there is not much to do or sometimes three or four journalists would be assigned with you and when we wrote up the story collectively, and at the end of the day, you get demoralized because whatever you add to the story, it is not that valued. Basically, there was a lot of discrimination at that time, if one can put it that way.
- During the liberation struggle it was also difficult to include the byline because we were protected, because then it was the struggle. So to be neutral, the byline was always "Staff Reporter". But on the other hand because the editor [Gwen Lister] knew the entire pros and cons she always put her name.
- At that time we were just concentrating on the politics and we had to put women issues aside. Until today it's been my dream to have a column with any newspaper [in Namibia] where I will talk about women's issues something that was difficult during the liberation struggle. During that time the concentration and focus was more on the struggle.

In my column I am thinking of talking about issues of HIV/AIDS, rape, abuse of women, the divorce rate in our country, financial stability... that women don't just need to depend on males to be financial independent... even general politics, diseases and a lot of other issues that we can share and educate the up coming generation. We need to educate each other.

- Gender inequality, one would not notice it so much at that time because the whole focus was on the struggle and there were not a lot of female journalists that one could compare. *The Republikein* was the only newspaper that had a more women journalists.
- You know, basically during the apartheid system you would go to the war zone and at one time we were flown to the war zone by the military and wrote a story on the PLAN fighters who were tight to the Caspers and we took some pictures. But whatever we wanted to cover, was monitored by the system. So, if you wrote something that did not go according to what they dictated to you, that's why you would always write a story and put "staff reporter". We went to cover an aftermath of a battle field between SADF and PLAN combatants.
- As a black woman journalist, my race affected me. And that is why I am not a journalist any more because if I had the support from those I was working with today, I could have been one of the top journalists today. I have inspired a lot of journalists like yourself, and the list is long. So, if I also had people who inspired me I was probably going to be one of the top journalists of this country, but I didn't have that support system. And if I was a black male journalist, I could have been in a better position because a lot of black male journalists still continue, but all black women journalists that worked as reporters during the liberation struggle are no longer practicing; Anna Erastus, a former black journalist she is now in fisheries... doing something totally different, Theodora Nandjaa, although she is with NBC [Namibia Broadcasting Corporation], she is now in advertising and marketing.
- What discouraged me from continuing is that there was no support. Gwen had all the opportunities, she could have even gone to the international community and solicit financial support to support me, as an up coming black woman journalist to study journalism and come back to the paper. We used to have journalists from abroad who would come and work at *The Namibian* for say six months, and they always tipped us off that we could get funding from the international community for further training abroad in journalism. So, I remember making that request to *The Namibian* but no body considered it. So you end up getting frustrated and if you get a better job offer elsewhere then you just leave. And that's what happened in my case. I quit and I went to translate at the court because

of my bilingual skills.
- You are a trainee journalist but then there was not much that you could contribute. If you have to contribute you have to go out on a story and in some cases the story is shared with the male journalists. And sometimes you are the one who brought the scoop. I remember when I was with *The Namibian* I was even appointed to be the BBC corresponded but it was heavily monitored by both the editor and the system. So I didn't have the liberty to talk to BBC.
- They [women] played a vital role. For instance, when the system [the regime] did not want to fly with male journalists then they took the women [journalists] because they felt it was easier to dictate to women, but us women, what we did was, we still came back and reported objectively and using the famous "staff reporter" as a byline. But of course the system would always find out [who could have written that particular story].
- We were there [in the media industry] because we loved to be there but there was no support.
- That time we were fearless warriors. We even thought that well, if you died during the liberation struggle it was going to be for a good cause. We were really fearless journalists. But then there was a lot of harassments, you had to watch where you were going. Like in town [city center] you would not just go there and socialize like now during independence and speaking your mind. During those days you were always scared that they could be hunting for you for the story that you wrote. Once I wrote a story on the controversial first April battle. The next morning an investigator from the South African regime was sent to come to *The Namibian* with a summon to appear in quote to testify about the story I wrote and I was scared to be locked up. But thank God the whole process of 435 [United Nations Resolution 435] came and the case just disappeared. I was about 25 years old then.
- I always went with my male colleagues because there were always some secret informants that would monitor our movements. The system didn't really respect women.
- I got in-house training at *The Namibian*.

Sue Cullinan

- I can't speak for Namibian women journalists in other news organizations, but *The Namibian* was established and run by women, so we did not experience gender-related constraints at the work place. The more difficult issue was juggling work and home, trying to raise children at the same time as hold down a full-time (and over-time!) job.
- We could report on anything we chose to, but the reality was that Gwen and I

(and later Jean) were tied to the office putting out the paper, so we did not travel to northern or war-torn areas but relied on stringers to cover those zones.
- We generally covered a story if it was a news story rather than making a special effort to write about women as a separate category. Fortunately there were several newsmakers around – Norah Chase, Ottilie Abrahams and others – so we would give them coverage. Perhaps male editors would not have given them such prominence, I don't know.
- I don't think we consciously brought a women's perspective into the news (Gwen's column was called 'political perspective' after all), but perhaps we saw things from a more humanistic point of view. We were as political as anyone else – probably more so – but being women, probably had a more encompassing, humanistic, view than men might have had.
- The fact that we had children (or others to support) and experienced, every day, the double shift that women work when they are supporting a family. It was also clear that the political choices we made were harder because they might affect the children (if we were detained or worse).
- I don't know but I hope so. SWAPO always said it would promote the rights of women but I'm not sure if that policy has been adequately fulfilled.
- The personal hostility we experienced was not so much from the press but from right-wing individuals and institutions who opposed change. Gwen and I were called "Swapettes" and other derogatory terms suggesting that we just political groupies rather than taking a political stand ourselves. I think *Die Republikein* published an ugly photograph of me one day with a story called "Toe daag Sue nie op" about some court case (I will look for the clipping). The pro-establishment press were always looking for a way to cast us in a bad light – especially Gwen – but it was political rather than gender-based. The fact that we were women might have infuriated them more.
- The apartheid system had a terrible effect on gender equality because it was based on a system of pass laws and migrant labour, which usually left women behind in remote areas trying to raise families with no income of their own, relying on remittances and with little chance of improving their lives. If there was a cultural bias in communities, the apartheid system reinforced it and made it very difficult for women to break through the gender barrier.
- Race was not an issue in our work place or how we performed.
- We made all the decisions ourselves and the Namibian is still edited by women so I guess gender equality would require bringing in a male editor or deputy!
- No, hardly at all in the other media (in Namibia) at the time.

- Yes, I believe we played a role in leading by example. The fact that we were determined to work in news, even with other responsibilities, showed that we were not only as good as anyone else (and better!) but that we could multi-task. It also showed that that politics was important to us and we needed to be involved at every level.
- Gwen and I had to take steps to protect our children from knowing we were being threatened and the offices of the Namibian were later bombed, so they had to take more security precautions than before. But the threat against us was political rather than gender-based.
- We were probably held in contempt by the white male community in Windhoek but that was not much of a price to pay. The main difficulty was the work/home balance as in point 1.
- I was given a basic training in radio news at Capital Radio in Johannesburg.
- We provided some training at the Namibian for journalists on the staff.

Carol Kotze

- I was born in South Africa but my parents are both Namibians. We came back to Namibia around 1951/52. So I grew-up in Namibia my whole life. I don't know why I wanted to be a journalist, but I had this thing about language and just enjoying working with language. So when I was in primary school, I started this newsletter when I was in grade five or there about, which I wrote on my own and I sold it at the school for one penny at the time. And that is in the 1950s that I am talking about. When I went to university, at the University of Pretoria, I did try to get a job as a journalist because then the interest was still there while I was studying for my degree. But then I couldn't get into it. I actually just got into it when I came back to Namibia in 1962 when I finished my degree. Then I got a job at an Afrikaans newspaper here in Windhoek called the Suidwester.
- I will first try answering these questions for you and then I am going to tell you this thing that I told you before about the dynamics inside the white population which really informed my experiences as a journalist. As I said to you before Maria, I am not a feminist. Your questions are very much focused on feminism, from a feminist point of view and in that way; I won't be able to really answer many of these things for you. But I will try, saying that because of my background as an English speaking Namibian, that made a big difference to my experience as a journalist. That brings me to this thing that I said about the dynamics inside the white population. The fact that white people are not all the same and we have this history between the English speaking Namibians and South Africans and the Afrikaans speaking Namibians and South Africans were the Afrikaners always, some

after the Anglo-Boer war, they accepted this idea that the English people oppressed them... that in fact, they have the right to run the country. After all they spilled their blood; this is how the propaganda went, in the Anglo-Boer war and before in their history, so it's their country. Now, in came the English, it became an English colony, in 1910 it became an English dominion and therefore the English were seen as the oppressors. And certainly when I was a child, we experienced this discrimination because we were English. The Afrikaners were in the process of removing the power from the English part of the population. They were busy empowering the Afrikaner through what we would now call in our modern terms as government parastatels. But of course they were organizations, banks and things like that which was started with the support of the government after 1948. They were specifically meant to empower the Afrikaner. And in this way, the English part of the population experienced what the white part of the population is now experiencing in Namibia, with the black people now empowering themselves, because they are in power, and they are removing the power from the white people, and trying to redistribute the wealth. Now this exercise, we have been through it before. Because the Afrikaans did this to the white English speaking people after 1948 as well. So these are the dynamics I am talking about.

- The relationship has not changed that much [between the Afrikaners, the English and the German communities in Namibia], because, except that the Afrikaner is finding himself again at the bottom of the white ladder if you like. Namibia has a very small English population.

- I was their [Suidwes] agricultural reporter which is a strictly male job I use to drive around the country to all the agricultural shows, I had to interview the farmers. I became quite an expert in agriculture, which is a male job. But I was educated... that makes the difference. Then I was their crime reporter, I had to go to all the murder scenes, suicides and things like that. They didn't treat me as a woman because I didn't insist on being treated as a woman. I became one of the boys. Meanwhile, the Afrikaans women were treated as women. They were sent on news assignments such as to cover the flower shows, women stories, which I am not slightly interested in, the cancer's association tea parties for instance, or welfare and other things like that. By then we didn't have any black reporters until after 1976. This year was the turning point when we were allowed to get rid of the apartheid laws, when we were allowed to start actually pulling in black people into our things, and then immediately it happened of course. Journalism is always far less conservative, even in a conservative newspaper it was far less conservative than other businesses. In 1976 I stopped working as a journalist because by then I had three children and couldn't continue running around to cover news. After other jobs such as teaching and lecturing, I went back to journalism in 1990 as editor at the *Times of Namibia*.

- People like Anna Erastus, she did something on women, which I had no problem with... but just don't ask me to do it.
- Gender inequality ... I must not make a sweeping statement; it depends on who you are. Some women cause their own inequality if you like. A woman who has, most white women in any case, and to certain extend 16 years after independence black women as well in urban areas, they have the chance to get educated. That is why I said they sometimes make their own inequality to a certain extend because they don't grab the chance.
- I was once a military correspondent, covering the war when I worked for *Die Republikein*. Once the newspaper sent me to cover the aftermath of a battle that had just taken place between the SWAPO soldiers and the South West Africa Territory Force in Angola. The military flew us from Windhoek in a Dakota into Angola.
- Obviously I wouldn't be able to do that because I couldn't write a story which was anti-government for instance because I worked for a paper that was pro-government. Just like I can imagine a person from *The Namibian* for instance would not report a pro-government article because they were anti-government newspaper. All newspapers tend to have their own agenda. There is nothing like an objective newspaper.
- I don't know if I can say whether in my writing I did [contributed to the liberation of the country], but certainly with my mouth. Because they all knew, I was accused very regularly by my own colleagues of being left, and a communist and a liberal and and "Kaffir Boetie" because I was the only one with black friends sitting down like with you [now]. So my colleagues looked at me with great suspicion.
- They [women journalists in Namibia today] certainly lack [feminist] awareness. But the problem will not be solved by a feminist movement. Because a feminist movement is seen by the male part of the population in many negative ways; they see it as that bunch of women together or a bunch of lesbians together. They have all these negative connotations about it. Whereas, I feel that this awareness must come from schools, education is the answer. The teachers must be sensitized... the teachers must be aware that girls are as good as boys. The problem in our country lies with the teachers. The teachers are not educated and that is a major problem. The teacher training in the country is very bad.
- By the time I went into journalism in 1963, I was already well educated as compared to other people in the journalism field. I suspect that I was one of the two or three people on the whole staff of the Suidwester who actually had a degree. My BA degree is in English and History. I did my other degrees, my honors degree and my master's degree and my doctoral degree; I did through UNISA.
- I have no training in journalism except in-house training which I believe is the right kind of training because it gets you into conduct with the nitty-gritty of what its

really about.
- When I went to work for *Die Suidwester*, I went as the only English speaking person on the staff of this newspaper. The point was, it is an Afrikaans newspaper, and my Afrikaans is very good, I was automatically given the job to translate from English to Afrikaans. I had to translate all the SAPA stories for instance into Afrikaans to put it in our newspaper, apart from also doing interviews.

Anna Erastus

- I was born in Walvisbay, Namibia were I did my primary education and I did my high school in the northern part of Namibia were I matriculated. And then from there I worked as a teacher, as you know the situation in Namibia then [as a black person] you were only suppose to be either a teacher or a nurse. Then I got married when I was very young. Then I went to Britain where I did a diploma in education and when I came back, I always wanted to be a writer, not much of a journalist, so when I came back... I don't think having obtained a diploma in education it was my desire to be a teacher so, I joined a local newspaper *[Times of Namibia*, in 1989] where I started to do some translations into a local language, and that's how I became a journalist.
- The environment was a male dominated one and it almost felt as though it was a privilege for a woman to become a journalist. So, obviously you are confined in that environment and sometimes you didn't even see that constraints [against women journalists] because you felt like you were done a favor to be in a male domain. If I can recall the environment I worked in by then, I was the only black woman and the majority of the other women who were there where white, and there wasn't much of a relationship between me and them...but we could make jokes about the men. We really never use to sit and discuss about issues that were really affecting us as women. Those women were even in a better position than me as a black woman...they were editors, and I was just a mere journalist. I knew at times, you could really see a lot of quarrels among the male and female whites. I can't really say what were the constraints because we never use to sit and discuss but I believe there where issues that I can not really pinpoint as such.
- I used to write a column mainly for women that was every Wednesday, and basically, I just used to cover more of women and children issues. Of course I could also do some other stories but my task was more to cover women, children and social oriented issues.
- I had to, actually, to fight for the column because a lot of women issues were coming up especially in Namibia, issues of gender were coming up, issues of representa-

tion of women in different institutions. That column made me a bit famous because that was the only newspaper with a column focusing on women issues by then. What I use to do, normally I would cover different kinds of issues, but I would always have a profile of these emerging women either as a parliamentarian or a woman in a financial institution. Not only prominent women but I was also looking at students, and grassroot women, just depending on what was emerging at that particular time and I would make it an issue.

- I think women issues in other media outlets were really not much considered.
- Like I said earlier, during that time a lot of women issues were coming up, but to what extend these issues were covered it was something else. Because that was the time when a lot of women organizations were coming up trying to sensitize women just after independence. But the coverage was very minimum.
- It is very difficult to talk about feminist in the Namibian context...there are a lot of women organizations. Now, whether you call them feminist organization, that is very interpretative. But of course I would say yes, there are a lot of women that are connected to different women organizations such as political organizations, financial, and women in business women organizations, social groups like lesbian women organizations, young women organizations and so forth.
- I think, gender inequality in a sense that women were not well represented in the institutions it was obvious by then and it's still obvious now but the difference is that there are a lot of institutional approaches to mainstream the gender in different institutions. There are also policies in place such as affirmative actions in government were they are trying to address the imbalances. Somehow they are trying to balance the situation but the inequality is still there.
- The apartheid system impacted on gender inequality on many aspects. First of all, a woman was never visible during that time. Women were excluded from many decision making processes.
- Like I said, I became a journalist because I wanted to be a writer but I didn't have the necessary skills to support my ability to perform to the fullest. Because of the apartheid system a lot of black people here were excluded from education and some of these professions or careers, they were not really open for black people for that matter. Because of that, it really constraints one's ability because to be a journalist you need to go through certain courses for you to understand how to write, how to approach people, how to do investigation and so forth and that you needed to learn. And in most cases [as a black journalist] you were always assigned to go for stories in the black community and never assigning you to broader issues that would include the white community. So its like they use to use black people, particularly the newspaper that I worked for, and it really

constrained you they used you for their own interest. But at the same time you learned a lot because you don't have the necessary qualifications, you don't have the skills, and you have not gone through a formal training, so it really affected you.

- I mean like I said, it was a male domain. During that time when I was a journalist, I never saw a black Namibian editor except in the government set-up like at the national broadcasting corporation. In most of the private media either if you see an editor is a white woman and most of them are not Namibians, either they are of South African or European origin. This just shows you that it wasn't that easy for a Namibian per se to be in a decision making position.
- I only became a journalist just before independence and during that period, I really tried to bring out issues concerning women... but there are women like Gwen Lister, we all know her... she really played a major role. She's been jailed and so forth.
- You know when I joined journalism I was very young and I was there just eager to learn. But I also had a lot of conflicts with male colleagues, always quarreling with them... because as far as they were concerned, you were just a woman. You were not supposed to question them. But I think if you want to survive as a journalist, you just have to be yourself, you need to know what you want, you have to be aggressive, and you don't need to compromise.... I guess just like any other professions, you just need to be very professional... but you also have to put across your point. By that time I was actually going into my 20s [age].

Lucy (pseudonym)

- I was employed by the South West African Broadcasting Corporation, SWABC, which became the Namibian Broadcasting Corporation, NBC, in Windhoek from 1 January 1989 to 31 July 1992. The general radio newsroom, to which I was initially assigned, was multiracial, multicultural and multilingual, comprising both male and female journalists. I was responsible for about seven news beats, including the arts, nature conservation, transport and water. However, I desperately wanted to cover the changing political landscape and dynamics in Namibia, which was in the international spotlight at the time. My news editor was a man and so too was the editor of the political team, which comprised white, Afrikaans-speaking male journalists, with the exception of one female journalist. When I indicated that I wanted to cover politics, my editor refused. I don't remember exactly what he said or why, but I don't recall it being gender-related. After much nagging on my part and persuasion from the political editor, my editor eventually agreed that I could cover politics, but on condition that I continued to cover all my other beats. This meant that I had to work harder and longer hours than most of my male colleagues. My first test came in February 1989 when I was assigned to cover Namibia's first-ever sport delegation to Angola, even though I was not a sports reporter. Despite some vocal resentment and unhappiness from one of my male sports colleagues, part of my brief was to secure an extensive interview with Swapo's representative in Angola, which I did. It was the first time in about 30 years that anyone from Swapo, which had been banned as a 'terrorist' organisation, was quoted and broadcast on national radio. My real break, though, came on the 1st of April 1989 when Swapo broke the UN-ceasefire. I was at Windhoek Airport for the arrival of an Angolan sport delegation. I was the only journalist who realised that Angola's Deputy-Foreign Minister, Venancio de Moura, was accompanying the sports delegation, and subsequently interviewed him about the ceasefire violation. I was also the only NBC journalist to stumble on South African Foreign Affairs Minister Pik Botha's angry news conference at the airport after he'd said goodbye to British Prime Minister Maggie Thatcher. I think my editors found it hard to ignore me – as an 'unguided missile', in their words, and as a young English-speaking female journalist, after this. Although I continued to cover the implementation of UN Security Council Resolution 435, the return of Swapo exiles and refugees, and Namibia's first-ever democratic election in the Caprivi, I was only officially appointed to the political desk in March 1990, shortly before Namibia's independence from South Africa. And if I remember correctly, it was only because the lone female political journalist had resigned. Following the appointment of Sam Nujoma as Namibia's first President, I remember my male colleagues suggesting that I cover the First Lady's 'tea parties' and women's meetings. I vehemently objected, saying that I wanted to cover the President, which I did, and that it would far more refreshing for them to cover his wife's activities. I mention all of this by way of example. I honestly don't believe that there was blatant gender discrimination. In fact, my short record of wonderful opportunities and my speedy promotion up the NBC ladder is proof of this. Rather, I think there was a lack of consciousness about what was possible and desirable in a brand new democratic country. I'm struck by the fact that not more female journalists wanted to or fought hard enough to cover the male-dominated beats of politics and economics, and also that the male editors didn't actively encourage more woman to embrace these subjects.

- As indicated above, I was initially assigned to cover about seven general beats, including the arts, nature conservation, transport and water, which is extremely important in an arid and drought-prone country like Namibia. But once I was allowed to cover politics, in addition to these beats, I covered most of the UN-related activities and developments; the return of Namibian exiles and refugees; the country's first-ever democratic elections from the Caprivi; Namibia's independence from South Africa; President Sam Nujoma's activities and statements; Namibia's foreign affairs and relations; State visits; meetings such as those of the former Frontline States; the future of Walvis Bay and the offshore islands; as well as Parliament. I covered these aspects for radio bulletins and current affairs programmes, and from March 1990, also for TV bulletins and special programmes. The reporting was factually based and pretty much down the line. Given the exposure I've since had to human-interest and creative radio storytelling, I shudder when I think of the kind of reporting I actually did. But that's the nature of experience and growth. When I was asked to supervise and co-ordinate NBC Radio's election coverage in the Caprivi, I was told that I wouldn't have to struggle speaking Afrikaans because it was an English-speaking area and also that it would be 'safe' compared to anticipated tension in Ovamboland. In fact, I ended up speaking rough and raw Afrikaans because the UN's Dutch contingent was deployed to the Caprivi. And the area proved not to be as 'safe' as NBC had imagined because Swapo troops were allegedly waiting in anticipation of the election outcome across the nearby Zambezi River.

- I remember initially making an effort to cover women's movements and their activities, but it was more politically related than anything else. Foreign Affairs Deputy-Minister Netumbo Ndaitwah was instrumental and extremely patient in gradually explaining liberation and African politics to me. I think and hope I applied the journalistic criteria of selecting or reflecting women interviewees and speakers, especially in Parliament, based on what they had to say, how they said it and the relevance. Now, I find that I subconsciously seek out women interviewees because they're natural storytellers, who don't often hide their emotions. My ears also prick up when I only hear a handful of women's voices and views in the news.

- I think my perspective was shaped by how I was brought up and who I am: A human being, a woman, racially classified as 'white' under apartheid, English-speaking with a Greek father and a South African-born Portuguese mother, curious, questioning and intolerant of abuse and injustice. I think my 'women's perspective' came out in the kind of questions I ask, for example, how do you *feel?* I think the voice and tone also shape a 'women's perspective'.

- Male and female attitudes and influences in my life, and probably 'the media' [influenced her gender-consciousness]. As the only daughter and eldest child in my family of three brothers, I remember my mom insisting that I wash the dishes on Sundays, while my one brother mowed the lawn. I couldn't understand why I couldn't mow the lawn now and then, or why I could only ride a *'dik weel'* bicycle when my brothers had 'racers'. But that's how my mom was brought up and that's how she thought she had to bring us up. Until I started questioning and challenging her, as well as the status quo in the world.

- I'm not formally connected to any feminist-orientated movement. In fact, I don't belong to any organisation or political party.
- I don't recall there being any blatant gender inequality in Namibia's media institutions. Instead, I recall women journalists, editors, managers and subs.
- When I arrived in Namibia, I was struck by the lack of apartheid and tension compared to South Africa. As I pointed out earlier, I entered a multiracial, multicultural and multilingual newsroom, with the exception of the political team. Although I initially found the easy-going human relations in Namibia strange, living and working there was a breath of fresh air! In my opinion, apartheid in Namibia may have existed in law, but in reality and in practice, it died a slow death a long time again. I clearly remember partying and dancing over the weekends in the 'black' and 'coloured' townships of Katutura and Khomasdal, rather than in town.
- I would be stupid and naïve to believe that my racial classification didn't affect my prism, approach to life and journalism. As indicated, I was born and bred in apartheid South Africa from 1966, about a week before Prime Minister HF Verwoerd was assassinated. Even though I was an English-speaking Catholic, born to 'second class' South Africans of Greek and Portuguese origin and grew up in a conservative Afrikaans town outside Johannesburg, I still had a lot more opportunities than the majority of 'black' South Africans. As a result, I had a lot more confidence. But this doesn't mean that I didn't have to fight or work hard for what I've achieved and accomplished. I guess I've learnt to wear obstacles and challenges – blatant or subtle – like a second skin. I don't easily take 'no' for an answer and I can't handle 'can't-do' attitudes.
- I didn't really encounter obstacles to decision-making responsibilities. As indicated, I was promoted very quickly at NBC. Within five months of my career, I went from journalist to sub-editor. In March 1990, I was appointed chief-sub-editor on the political desk. Later in 1991, NBC's Director-General and its News Controller appointed me as Acting TV Bulletin Editor. And in January 1992, I was promoted to TV Foreign Affairs Senior Producer – a post I held until my resignation. Because I was exposed to so much at such a young age and early stage in my career, I've resisted management and prefer to stay in touch with 'real people' in the field, doing what I love best – newsgathering and storytelling. The unofficial initiatives that I've taken are to mentor and encourage young female journalists.
- Initially, the NBC Director-General, News Controller, and radio editors of general news, current affairs, bulletins and politics were all men. So, the top level was male-dominated. Women featured as radio bulletin shift editors, currents affairs producers and presenters, chief-sub-editors and sub-editors, as well as TV bulletin editors etc.

- I believe and hope I played a significant role in the creation of Namibia as a democratic country. It was exciting to witness, document, report on and be part of the transformation and change. My Namibian experience was definitely an excellent training ground and precursor for my role in the transformation of South Africa and the South African Broadcasting Corporation, SABC.
- Challenging myself and others; not taking 'no' for an answer; pushing myself hard to do my best; stretching boundaries; under-promising and over-delivering; willing to experiment and fail and try again; squeezing playtime, free-time and friends into hectic schedules and deadlines etc.
- As indicated earlier, I had to work harder and longer hours to prove myself, to myself, my colleagues and my bosses even though they never said they required or expected that of me. I also don't think there was any support for female journalists who were also mothers. Many had to quietly juggle their maternal roles and responsibilities with their journalistic careers.
- Before working as a journalist, I obtained a one-year post-graduate diploma in journalism and media studies from Rhodes University in Grahamstown. NBC also arranged a one-week, I think, orientation course, before we actually started working...in the real world.
- As indicated above, NBC provided a one-week orientation course for us before we actually started working. I remember being shown how to edit good-old fashioned tape on the reel-to-reel machines and also getting some voice/presentation training. In 1990, the Friederich Ebert Foundation selected and sponsored me to participate in the annual two-month United Nations Training Programme for Broadcasters and Journalists from Developing Countries in New York, USA. Other than that, everything I learnt, I learnt on the job, from my colleagues and from trial and error.
- Unfortunately, I don't have any copies of my stories from Namibia, but given my dates of employment and the nature of your study, I'm sure you could request archival recordings or dubbings directly from NBC.

Rene Lötter

- I ended-up here quite by accident. I studied at Stellenbosch University [South Africa], studying literature and psychology. In those days Stellenboch was regarded as the pot beat of Afrikaans nationalism. It was suppose to be the university where all the new young leaders are being primed but that's not how we came out. Somehow we came out as everything but nationalism. We came out very critical. I came to Namibia because it was the transition time, it sounded like a good idea. It sounded like an interesting place. I wanted to work here for like a year, I ended up staying much longer. I came here in 1987... and I started my media career at the State Broadcasting, the South West Africa Broadcasting Corporation (SWABC). I stayed for quite a few years, maybe five years, and then I left for the *Times of Namibia* – it no longer exists. That was around independence where everybody expected to bloodbath that but everything went very smoothly... It wasn't really a revolution.

- [Speaking about gender constraints]You had to put your foot down and speak up if you wanted to be taken seriously. Women were expected to be seen and not heard. Subservient. Only if you were aligned with a man via marriage or if your dad was a powerful figure you would get more esteem. So if you wanted to be heard during office meetings instead of getting blank stares, you had to state your case clearly and assertively. The girls in the office knew Margaret Thatcher was politically not kosher at the time but boy, did we try and emulate her style when dealing with the big boys. (Please note I am talking about the state media here.)
- There was a lot of coverage on the bush war. We were not allowed to use the Swapo word too often, in fact, sometimes they were counted. The editors closely scrutinized every insert. Women out in the field covering "tough assignments" were in the minority. Women were mainly desk bound subs and presenters.
- I cannot remember anything specific [about whether women journalists made any efforts to cover women and women's issues in their stories] except *Sister Namibia* [magazine] that was aimed at grassroots women.
- I don't know how effective [women organizations in Namibia are], I get the impression that there are fewer strong women around these days than during the struggle days!
- [In newsrooms] men who got married and started families were blatantly promoted (jumped) past their female colleagues with more experience and skills. Nowadays enforced Affirmative action laws prevent this, but the mentality is still very well entrenched.
- [On the impact of the] divide and rule: Women were expected to dress and behave in a certain way and they did. They also did not exactly unite and plot insurrection to "emancipate themselves from this mental slavery".
- Most women I know and worked with did not believe that anything affected their ability. Not until they were brainwashed by their superiors and allowed their self-confidence to be undermined.
- I was not very impressed with the spirit of unity among women. I found lots of evidence for the old stereotype of – whenever a woman was in line for promotion the

other women would undermine her, and side with "the enemy".

- [On whether women journalists were represented at decision-making levels of the media:] Not really unless they started their OWN media outlets or were puppets put in place because they were easily handled.
- [On whether she believes she played a significant role in the liberation struggle as a journalist:] Well, in the state media machine those days … only by thinking: "At least I am in this position and can tone down the propaganda since I am not enthusiastic about the cause". If another person was in this position she/he may have spread worse or more damaging lies [about the struggle]. And at least sometimes one could be just a little subversive.
- [On what survival mechanisms, if any, women journalists employed:]Alcohol abuse! No serious, at the time we all felt that we were in the same boat – "hoernaliste" not "joernaliste". We all felt like we were prostituting our talents. Some "leaked" stories to the outside world. Others "disappeared" features or inserts. We became experts on the different nuances bias and emotion the subtle use or omission of certain adjectives and adverbs evoked. In a strange way, many years later, this skill of subtly manipulating opinion by just tweaking words here and there, have made me a good spin doctor.
- [On whether there was an organized feminist agenda in the newsrooms]No. There was no formal feminist agenda.
- Women constantly had to fight against being treated with just a little bit of "Yes dearie okay let's hear your cute little opinion, if we must".
- I came into the [media] field with a related degree, yes.
- [On whether the media institution she worked for provided her with any formal training in journalism], Yes, very good training on a certain level.

Estelle de Bruyn

- I was born in 1958 in South Africa. I started my journalistic carrier at a newspaper in Johannesburg, South Africa. And fell in love with a guy who moved to Namibia and I followed him in 1981. And then we got married, I got a job at SWABC. And I had a son and I worked there and I did all the horrible little jobs that no one else wanted to do. Like the medical beat, and the educational beat, things like that. I worked for TV at the time, and then in 1989 when 435 came about, I have always wanted to do politics and I begged them to put me on a political desk. And I succeeded, and I am very grateful for that because I covered, it was the most fantastic experience, the whole run-up to the elections and the writing of the constitution, and the independence. By that time my husband had died and

I got a job offer to go to South Africa. So I joined the SABC in Pretoria, remarried and then I had a wonderful opportunity to cover the whole South African democratization process again, and did the whole constitution writing (reporting) in South Africa again. And this whole experience in Namibia really was a wonderful background, because the journalists in South Africa didn't know what to expect and all. It really gave me an urge which was wonderful. In 1997 I returned to Namibia. But I am too old for TV now. I joined *The Republikein* and I have been here since.

- [On gender-related constraints in the Namibian newsrooms during the liberation struggle:] I don't know, I can only speak for myself, but initially the only journalists who did politics were men, they had no problem with me doing military, for instance, but politics... that was the domain of men. I went out during the war and they had no problem with that, but they didn't think women could really understand politics because all politicians were more or less males at the time. And then 1989 came and I said I really wanted to do politics and they said okay. So I don't think I experienced really biased, I just accepted it at the time but when I really wanted to do it, they gave it to me. I just think they were glad that any person would want to do it [reporting on military affairs] because they were too lazy to go out [and cover military events]. It was one of those things that the defense force at the time would take journalists to the north, [the war zone] to press conferences, or into Angola to see the operations there. My ex-husband at the time worked for the *Republikein*, so it was always nice to go out together and do these things. I remember there was this Operation Protea, it was a military operation into the South of Angola and it was, we were on this side, Swapo was on this side, and they [SWAPO] were the enemy and we went in and they [the South African Defense Force] showed us some military vehicles that were shot at, luckily we did not see any dead people and I am very glad for that. But one of the nicest stories that I covered was after the First of April, 1989 incursion. I was also sent to the north [to cover] the handover of the prisoners that were taken. And that was also very exciting.

- Before I became a political journalist, as I said, women were mainly doing education and arts, and medical things and the city council and things like that. But when I look at people like Gwen Lister for instance, she has always been into the politics and she had the run to do, and the capacity, and the intelligence, and the drive. And, for instance, if I think of the girls in our newsroom, they all just sat there and look pretty on TV, and none of them pursued a career in journalism like I did. They all got married and now teaching somewhere.

- Gender was never an issue at that time. We never had a gender agenda. We never thought of women as a target group that needed to be covered and things like that. Women were more like presenters.

- The first time that I became aware of gender issues and that it was important it was after independence, and that was with very strong women returning from exile, like Pendukeni [Ithana], and like [Netumbo] Ndaitwah, and Libertine [Amathila]. We were amazed. It was because they were so strong... they really pushed the gender issues. And it was for the first time I realized that gender was an issue. I think now there is a gender consciousness, but then on the other hand, I have always struggled to be treated equal. And if I wanted to be treated equal I can't always be saying I am a woman I need special favors. Especially in a male dominated newsroom like this *[Die Republikein]*. You know what, the young women journalist of today they get send out to do the gender issues; the women's action for development and rights... because when I was on the political desk, I was the only woman and they never treated me any different. We got the stories at the beginning of the day and there was never an issue that because you are a woman you must do this. They treated me so equal, it was wonderful for me. It was a very special group of men that I worked with. They were all married; they had happy families, and their wives worked and all. But they treated me like a colleague. I had kids at that time. There were no lee ways, if my kids were ill, then sorry. You were a journalist; this is not a soft job. So I had to make other arrangements to take care of my son. These days it's a lot softer and they are gentler and when you don't have a baby sitter that day they could let you bring the baby to the office. Those days it was unheard off. Now in the *Republikein*, they have more women journalists. There were very few women journalists at SWABC.
- I have not been interested [in feminist movements] maybe because of the same philosophy that I don't want to be treated differently because I am a woman. Equal treatment is fine. I have not felt the need to associate or perhaps belong to an organization to be protected, because I feel comfortable in the way that my career has gone in which my gender has not affected my career.
- It was not really blatant [gender inequality], as I said, when I wanted a career move, I could make it. They actually asked me to make a documentary program for them [SWABC management at the time] to asses my ability, my political savvy on the program. And I made a program in 1989 saying why Walvisbay should be included in the independence of Namibia. And they just said okay, you can do it, you can now be on the political desk. And I don't think they just tested me because I was a woman but because I was only doing soft news and they didn't know my capability.
- I think the apartheid thing really impacted on black women, I was not affected but for instance, I think its only been about 3 years ago that we had the first black female colleague here [at the *Republikein*]. And probably because of the language [the *Republikein*

is published in Afrikaans]. Also at SWABC there were no black women who applied to be journalist. In Radio there were women but there were black presenters and they were also black female producers in the magazine side of the broadcasting. But there were no black female journalists. I never saw their applications at the time. I can't think of a black female journalist at *The Namibian* either at the time or at *The Observer*. They were very few. I can't think of going out on a story with a black female reporter, it's weird. But now things have changed because if I now look at for instance NAMPA *[Namibia Press Agency]* and *New Era*, there are incredible competed journalists that are black women.

- I never felt a black politician would not talk to me because I was white. When I did experience a bit of restrain was when I came back from South Africa in 1997. Then a lot of the politicians had changed. There were only a few of the old guys who remembered me. But the new guys... it really took some time to build confidence and to gain their trust. And the amazing thing is that I did an interview with a very prominent politician a few years ago... and he was very reserved and I did a profile on him.

- In those days, we were not allowed to join any unions, it was out the question. And there were no women in top management [of SWABC], it was in this whole totalitarian control mechanism of management that they had at a time.

- [On whether women journalists were represented at decision-making levels of the media] Not on top management. But, for instance, on our political desk, if I remember correctly, I think we were six, with an editor (all men), and they included me in decision making.

- [On whether she believes she played a significant role in the liberation struggle;] I didn't, I was working for the government broadcaster. I don't think I played any role. The only role that I might say to my self was a reconciliatory role. When the retainees came back, when we had to alleviate the fears of the white people in the country... who were saying oh gee all these bad guys coming from exile; they are going to take over the country. [We had] to explain the role of democracy, to bring peace, to tell people that you know what; no matter who wins this election the sun will rise tomorrow... you will stay in the house... your kids will go to school, there is nothing to panic about... if you are a democrat you will also accept the results of the elections if you lose. I think, perhaps in that sense, I might have played a small role.

- I have always felt connected to my male colleagues... we were all alienated from the bosses, but as a group, the journalist males and females; we supported each other. There was never anything that I felt I had to do to prove myself to survive or to protect myself.

- I had a BA degree and one of my subjects in my first year was communication science... I always wanted to be a journalist but I taught first. And then I worked for the student newspaper. I started my first job as a journalist in South Africa.

• I don't see it [a vibrant feminist movement in Namibia], but I can be wrong. But I always feel women don't need to be educated... we need to educate the men they are the people who discriminate, they don't see our values, we know who we are. We are very happy to be who we are. They need the gender sensitive training, and things like that.

Rianne Selle

• I was born in South Africa I went to school there. But I never was really interested in the media but I did a degree in Latin and French and a teacher's diploma. In 1976, I came to Namibia and got a job at a newspaper. And in 1986, I returned to management of media in the then government service with the department of governmental affairs. Since then I have been in the media but more from a management point and more as a development communicator.

• Well, during the 1970's and the 1980's there was no way you would get a woman as an editor unless they owned the newspaper. For instance, there were only two or so women editors Carol Kotze, is a good example, she was working in *The Republikein Group* and they started the *Times of Namibia*. But despite her having a History degree and an English degree a man got a post over her. And that's when she left the media. But then the only other women editors were at the Namibia - Gwen Lister, who started the newspaper and owns it. Then there was *Abacus* editor, Heidi [von Egidy], who was later tragically killed in her flat [in Windhoek]. And those were the only women editors you saw in publications. Except perhaps in the government service, but then again we were very strong women. For instance, I left some newspaper in 1977 because my male colleagues got increases and got promoted, and I didn't. So I take it that it was because I am a woman. Then I joined *The Windhoek Advertiser.* I soon left the paper again because of the male attitude. That was in 1978 then I went to a private sector. There was definitely not many opportunities, on the other hand, unlike in South Africa where your beats were really more aligned to male/females, for instance it was really unlikely for a woman in the 70's to be a military correspondent [in South Africa]. In Namibia, with the small newspapers that we have here and the small number of stuff, that could happen. And I, in 77 and 78 served as a military correspondent for *The Windhoek Advertiser*.

• During that time news was definitely controlled. You focused on what the military wanted you to focus on. If you are flown into the military areas you would go where they wanted you to go, and you will get military briefing.

- Guerilla fighters were generally thought as terrorists, some farmers were killed in Otjiwarongo... you go up with your own car, but then the military still have the command and you are stuck with their briefing. The only people that really got the people's stories were *The Namibian,* and they had to work under bare circumstances. Gwen Lister was held up in the airport; the Namibian people were in the fear of arrest; tear-gassed. In 1978, I was told by one of my conducts in the military that I must watch it, I am considered a danger. Then I went to one of the PR guys at the military and said, hey, what is this I hear that I am not to be trusted? And then immediately, I was summoned to the military headquarters were a colonel interrogated me as to who told me that the military considered me a danger. They wanted the name of my conduct but I wouldn't tell them. And after that, I was sort of *persona non grata* with the military, and I didn't get their favored scoops, which didn't really disturb me at the time. I left the media soon after that.

- [On the coverage of women's issues:] I think prior to independence there wasn't that much. Some newspapers usually had a women's page, which looked at beauty and house hold issues like cookery... and things like that. And they would cover the women's agricultural union and things like that. The only time when women really read the newspapers in the 70s and 80s was if there was some scandal or so. It was only after independence that there was a change. And I think a lot of changes come from the United Nations, the international world. Because internationally we were quite far behind the women of the 60s, feminism... and it's only after independence, when SWAPO came back, having participated in the world conference on women in Nairobi and so on. Because in pre-independence [Namibia] the interim government of Namibia was not acknowledged. And of course it could not participate in all these conferences. So after independence, the government was fully recognized internationally because they had already, as a liberation movement, attended these international conferences. And that is when the whole convention of the elimination of all discrimination of women started being taken into Namibia. An example is our constitution in 1989, where previously no body will have thought of women being discriminated against and that we need affirmative action for women. But for instance, like I said, in 1986 I joined the Interim government and I was Head of the publication division. We had one monthly newspaper... and then we had a regular publication coming out every two weeks on record. We took from the newspapers the main stories about Namibia and we published them, and that is what is on the record in the media in Namibia or in South Africa about Namibia. There was such discrimination in the government service. First of all, at that time they had equal salaries in the government service, but a married woman did not qualify for a housing loan even if the husband didn't have such a facility. But an unmarried woman, unmarried man, divorced woman, divorced man, married man qualified. I was married in 1986 I got divorced on paper from my then husband because I didn't qualify for a housing loan and he didn't have a loan facility... I was seven months pregnant with my second son. And we got married and divorced on paper because of that discrimination. When we wanted to publish a newspaper article about discrimination in the interim government, against women, they refused for the article to be published. Although I tried to make them understand that I [was forced to] divorced my husband on paper to enable me to get a house.

- I do think there is much more [feminist] awareness, and if you look at publications such as *The Namibian*, I really look at the name to be more of an ideal of what the media should be, generally. If you look at that article of a woman selling "Kapana" (food sold in the street) on the road ... and making a whole article about that woman and writing on how she supplements her income and what the money goes to, you don't find that in any of our news media. *New Era*, I think its trying but I think they just don't have the interest.

- It was very blatant [gender equality]. It was absolutely blatant. If you look at the SWABC...I joined the SWABC in 1982... my son was born... he was six months when SWABC was looking for a journalist working from home to do a bulletin on Radio and Television. Television came into Namibia in 1976, and I wanted to publish a radio bulletin. I started doing this for them from home. Radio and Television came out weekly. And I worked part time from 1982 until 1984. I resigned end of 1984 when I was working half day already. Because of this job, I knew what was happening in the SWABC. All the managers there were men only, its was only just before independence [in 1990] when one woman made it into management of the English service at the Radio. But, there were just no opportunities for women to advance at the SWABC.

- [On whether women tried to do anything at all to change the discrimination:] I resigned, I went into corporate world. There wasn't such awareness of this discrimination. Because we weren't part of the international instruments as we are after independence. So that does play a role if you have that awareness. Just before independence, when we had a lot of international media here, then you had a lot of strong women who were covering the Namibian independence process and pre-independence. Even the local women journalists [during the independence process] came out much stronger.

- There has been a lot of [sexual] harassment of women journalists that we all know.

- I don't think Namibia is a country where you find these movements [feminist] so strong. [Feminist] awareness is there, but I do think that we address it in a different way. For instance, the Women's Action for Development, the only reason they are successful is that, number one, they have a very strong leader there but they are focused on helping women; to empower women. Veronica De Klerk is the leader. Whereas NANAWO, the only time they meet is when there is something political or something. Whereas even Namibia Women's Association of Ottilie Abrahams, that women organization has not really gone far after independence. Whereas the Girl Child organization is doing well...so I don't see an organization on gender successful if they don't have a strong focus on training. We need to speak out. The only time you hear of NAMWA for instance [Namibia Media Women's Association] is when a funder wants to come in and help them or when they have an annual general meeting, or they have to submit a report. I am a founder member of NAMWA and I believe young women should take up the struggle...Even MISA Namibia, you hardly here from them. And the Media Council of Namibia... brilliant idea but nothing is happening.

- Look, I think now the sky is the limit. In our government service, the Ministry of Information and Broadcasting is probably one of the best aligned in the whole of government service with affirmative action but if you look at NAMPA and *New Era*, for instance, there is no gender balance on management levels... that's why you hear more stories there of sexual harassment.

- [On whether women journalists played a significant role in the liberation struggle:] I think yes and no. I don't think at your mainstream media you would have found that so much. But you found it at *The Namibian*, I think if it wasn't for Gwen Lister, Jean Sutherland and all those other leaders there, we would not have seen the reports of what was really happening in this country in the North [the war zone]. They were the first to report the atrocities, when the military would just flatten a homestead; when they suspected they there were SWAPO soldiers there... I think *The Namibian* played a major role. In the government service, we had a policy that we would not write about the military.

- There was a general perception that women had to exchange sexual favors with their male bosses in order to work in that environment. And I think that perception still holds true.

- I got on the job training [in journalism].

Theodora Nandjaa

- When I finished my grade 12, I got a desire to be a journalist after I read newspapers and I got inspired to join journalism. After graduating from high school, I came to Windhoek at the CCN (Council of Churches in Namibia), which was the only progressive institute in Namibia, in a search for a scholarship in 1987. They first had to train me before they could get me a scholarship. So in the meantime I worked for the CCN newsletter. It used to give information about Namibia. It used even to be send to Namibians in exile.

- Although the kind of news we use to cover were really church related, not all were though we could also pick up any news item which we deemed relevant to the Namibian population and also abroad. But to come to your question, you know, it was not per se gender [inequality] but really human rights, I think. But one can also argue that, human rights were not respected in Namibia, let alone gender. So gender was not really a priority by then, people were more concentrating on human rights. Gender was really a secondary issue.

- [On the kind of assignments women covered;] I can give an example of myself, there were Namibian women, they had a problem because the South African army camps were close to the schools, they were strategically placed close to the schools where there were hostels [in northern Namibia]. And that was done specifically so that when the freedom fighters wanted to attack the army camps, they would not do that because there were schools. There was an incident in the northern Namibia were a certain army camp was attacked. As a result some bullets spill into one school and some school kids also got killed. So the Council of Churches in Namibia organized women from the CCN women's wing to petition to headmen Weulu in Oukwanyama, were that camp was close to. And because I happened to be a woman I was sent to go with these women to write a story and obviously CCN did not want to be seen sending a journalist right, so because I was a woman I went pretending that I was also part of that group that went to petition. But in the meantime, of course I was a young girl, I could not be classified as one of the mothers but in the meantime I was part of them. The mothers and I wrote then that story when the women went to petition the headman. That was around 1988. [Theordora was about 21 years old then.]

- What happened that day was that, the head man did not take it really lightly that women came to petition him that the camp must be taken away because the headman happened to have been supporting the South African regime. And he started insulting those women and the women started crying and me who was supposed to be a journalist, I also started crying. So, that is an incident I remember which I was assigned to because I was a woman, because I accompanied other women [gone undercover].

- As I said ealier, I think during that time the issue was really about human rights, which was not respected and women's rights happen to be part of human rights. As we all know women were part and parcel of the struggle. I don't think there was really a special attention/agenda to cover women issues. The priority was really human rights and not so much on women.

- In my case. I was almost the only journalist at the newsletter. I was a kind of a trainee journalist. [Theodora liaised only with the editor at the time, Daniel Tjongarero and

the photographer.]
- I don't think feminism is a big issue in Namibia. I remember at one point I was sent to a workshop in Zimbabwe by my previous employee, *New Era* [after independence of Namibia]. It was aimed at reporting on women issues but I think since I left *[New Era]* I don't think any Namibian women journalists were sent to that workshop again, because that one sensitizes you to be gender conscious.
- I think, except for the private media, *The Namibian,* which at that time had women reporters such as Gwen Lister who was the editor few others had women. I know that the other media were male-dominated. Like in all other professions, Namibian black women, except from being a nurse of teacher, were not really exposed to other professions. So that could be the reason why they were also not many in journalism. Women in Namibia were confined to teaching and nursing. Other fields were really not open to them. It was just something that was really discouraged and maybe they [women] could not also see themselves doing that. But if you look from the background of the girl child, its like, they have not really been promoted or uplifted at the same level as their male counterpart.
- Journalism has even been more like a reserved field, perhaps one can say, for whites. But again, we must understand that the first private press and more open to blacks was *The Namibian* which started in 1985, but otherwise before then, you could not be a journalist then. A journalist doing what? Reporting where? Unless you really supported the status quo. You can not compare it with nursing obviously, but as a nurse you go and be a nurse in the hospital. But fine you can study to be a journalist but then doing what? Until an independent paper came up. Media was really used as a propaganda tool to oppress our people. So unless if you wanted to be involved in this propaganda, only then could you be a journalist. Otherwise, as I said, before 1985, if you wanted to be a journalist and you don't support the regime of the time then you would really not have any work to do. Unless, if one joined a newspaper like the CCN Newsletter but its capacity to take journalists was also very small.
- The issue of mixing black and white people it was not there. And obviously if you were a black person and going to go to a white gathering they would obviously identify you as a black and a journalist but obviously if Gwen, for instance, went there, she could not have much of a problem.
- I think like in the case of *The Namibian* women were in managerial positions because the paper was and still is owned by Gwen who is a woman. Today, like at the NBC [where Theodora currently works] for example news and current affairs is headed by a woman and the second in command is also a woman. In Namibia, the fact that one is a woman does no longer prevent you from climbing up managerial positions. I know for

example in Zambia, were I practiced a bit [of journalism], you couldn't find really even a woman editor or a subeditor in the newsroom. I don't think women were taken seriously in Zambia either. I am convinced that there is some level of gender equality in Namibia now. The gender issue is really being addressed in Namibia. People in Namibia are really becoming gender sensitive, whatever decisions they take they don't sideline the women unless if one doesn't really have the capability to perform the job. I think affirmative action is also playing a role.

- I believe women like Gwen Lister, for example, they played a significant role of informing the world out there about the brutalities of the South African forces in Namibia on ordinary citizens. I think that is the role they *[The Namibian]* really played, and whatever small it was, women really played a role. *The Namibian* newspaper, which was established by a woman and the first independent publication in the country which was then read all over the world about the situation in Namibia, I think it really played a role.

- I think from what I could pick up, female journalists like the Sarah Johannes [Damases], you really had to be tough and extra ordinary, not just your women in the streets. You really had to put up with insults from people you would go to interview. They would disrespect you as a woman since you ventured in a field that is really a male domain.

- I started as a trainee journalist at CCN. They later got me a scholarship from the World Council of Churches, based in Geneva. So, I got a one year scholarship to be trained as a journalist in Zambia at the Africa Literacy Center in Kitwe. I came back [to Namibia] and joined *New Era* in 1991, and then later went to *Namibia Review* and then NBC. [She is now in the advertising and marketing department of NBC.]

- There is another worth mentioning event which I went to cover also in the northern part of Namibia. The freedom fighters attacked a South African army camp during the night and in the process, one young civilian man was killed in his homestead who was just caught up in a fight. So I went from Windhoek to the North with my camera and then the South African forces came to a place and started beating up people and intimidating them and asking the masses if they had seen freedom fighters around. Then I had my camera hanging up on my neck, a note pad, this was in 1988 when the war was really hot. It was black soldiers (Koevoet) and they saw my camera and a note pad, so they started beating me up. Here was now a journalist in the village and I was beaten, I was the only one who was beaten up. And there were people who admired me for being a journalist but here I was crying being beaten up. But people really pitted me, in the end I was really embarrassed but I am sure I only cried because I was a woman. I don't think a male journalist would be beaten up and cry openly, but I mean that weakness of being a woman it came out. But I was the only person they beat up but purely because they might have known everybody in the village. They could see that I was like a stranger... it was in my village, Oshipaya. So I was beaten up on my way to cover the event. I think I was beaten up maybe because of the camera. But I don't think they could have beaten up a male journalist like that although they use to do it. I know I was really beaten up because I was a young female stranger in the village with a camera.

Carmen Honey

- I grew-up in South Africa in a town called Bloemfontein. When I left school my dream was to become a journalist and there was only one job in our town and I didn't get it. So I went to work for a public library for a few years and traveled. When I came back I was able to work in the library of the newspaper, and after a short while of working in the library the editor came to fetch me saying I didn't belong in the library. Then I got my job. I was there I worked for a couple of years first as a journalist and then a photographer. In fact I was the second woman, ever in South Africa, to take newspaper pictures officially. Then I had children and I wasn't working for several years, and in 1985 I went back to work at *The Windhoek Advertiser* [in Namibia]. And then in 1988, I joined *The Observer*, *The Windhoek Advertiser* staff had walked out and I was with them. And in 1989 I was offered a job by the *South African Press Association* (SAPA) to beef-up their staff in Windhoek because independence was coming and they needed more people. So from 1989 to 1993 I worked for SAPA which was very interesting and exciting. And then I went to join the educational project, ABACUS, and we had to stop that in 1995 and I came to *The Namibian*.
- [On gender inequality:] The only gender bias I found at one stage, I can't remember the year, was when a South African war ship had to go up the coast to Angola or beyond to rescue people. I can't remember if it was a war situation or a natural disaster, but because I was a woman I wasn't allowed to go on the ship... that was the only gender issue that came to my work that I was prevented to do something because I was a woman. In my experience there was no holding back because I was a woman, at least not in the institutions that I worked at anyway. It's always been a bit of criticism that not enough women. I think no one has been that consciousized to women's issues, we didn't worry so much about women issues we were more worried about people's issues considering the situation [war situation] that was going on at the time. We didn't consciously or not consciously cover women's issues. We were simply doing the jobs we were given to do. Its just now after independence that we look back and see that there wasn't much done about bringing women perspectives into the news. There wasn't much of a gender consciousness.

- I don't belong to them [feminist movements] and I don't have an intention to join them because I think our work is wider than that. We cover women's issues, children's issues, people's issues all the time. They [feminist organizations] are probably out there but I don't know much about them. There could be a need for feminist-oriented because if we look at some of the things that Colleen Lowe Morna brings to our attention, maybe that necessarily because maybe we get caught up in our own stereotypes.
- I don't think there has ever been blatant inequality. If you look at my current organization [The Namibian] its women heavy if any thing... I can only speak for that.
- Well, apartheid kept people out of things, but it didn't only keep women out of things, it kept everybody out of things. I don't think a lot of women were any lot worse than the men. But it did affect black women and black people in general.
- We actually are very lucky in this country, I have never seen anyone being stopped because they were women and certainly not because they were black women. However things happened a lot in this country in the 1970s and in 1985 when I went to work, there weren't many black women but they were certainly doing their thing. I don't know if the institutions were holding them back such as the SWABC and other publications but in my experience I saw everybody out there doing their job.
- Now, women in general are not adequately represented. We have made a bit of a start, and the government talks about 50/50 but we still have a long way to get there. For instance we don't have enough women in parliament but I again we want women of caliber; we don't want them to be there just because they are women. They must earn their place there.
- [On whether she believed women played a significant role during the liberation struggle:] My editor Gwen Lister, for instance, is one person who played a huge role, and continues to play a big role. She happened to be there and she used her position to do all sort of all sorts of things.
- I think the nature of the job held many women back in those days. A lot of women had kids and they were married and their husbands could not let them going all over the country at the funny hours and so. I don't think they were particularly gender held but it was just sort of an inconvenient sector, so they took jobs with fix hours such as subbing, they didn't go out there covering stories as much. But I think there were quite a few of them doing the fix-hour jobs. That's my impression anyway.
- [Women] had to be tougher than people out there when they went to do their job out there in the in the streets and other tough places.
- I got an in-house training at my first newspaper job in Bloemfontein, South Africa.

Jo Rogge

- I came to Namibia in 1986 and I worked in the print industry [Multi Services], so I didn't enter through journalism directly but through my interest in publications. That was my entry point into journalism. The first publication that I was really involved with was the starting of *Sister Namibia* in 1989 with Estelle Coetzee.

- As you know it was the time before independence and a lot of activism around resolution 435 at the time in the country and we were involved with that on a political level. The motivation for starting *Sister Namibia* was the fact that there were no publications looking specifically at women's issues and if there were women's specific issues being looked at in the mainstream media, it was mainly around beauty tips and consumer news on that kind of level. It wasn't looking at gender issues specifically. So we felt that there was a lacking in that area and together with one of the UNTAG personnel, a woman who was a Director of UNTAG in Okahandja, who was responsible for Otjozondjupa region. She was a very strong feminist activist. And through my connection with her and my discussions with her, the idea for *Sister Namibia* grew out of that. She had come from Cuba.

- From my personal experience in the organization I was working in, for example, we were not allowed to travel out of Windhoek without male colleagues, which was a constraint clearly because you were stuck in the office until such time that they could accompany you to where you wanted to go. We were doing media work, and in this case we were producing publications. And we had to then be escorted by male colleagues, for whatever reason. So, that I saw as a constraint.

- Women were not sent out on hard news stories... I don't believe. From the coverage of the media at that time, where it was related to gender issues, as I said, it was on beauty tips, you didn't hear about women being involved politically, that wasn't reported very much. And that's why, with the run-up to the elections, Sister Namibia (in its first publication) then started to look at some of the women that were running for office. We looked at the women that were represented in different political parties. This was in a number of the first issues, from 1989 to 1990.

- There were very few women journalists at the time who did anything more than 'soft' news. I don't think there was any [gender consciousness], there may have been individual's working who may have, in the course of their political work had come into conduct with the terminology and the issues around gender or some feminist issues or whatever, but I don't believe that it was mainstream at all.

- I would say [gender inequality] was blatant, purely also because there wasn't gender consciousness, so it was almost as if that role's stereotyping was in place without anybody questioning it because there wasn't a consciousness for people to question it. So if women were not being assigned to the kinds if stories that they maybe would have like to be doing, they didn't question it because there wasn't a consciousness because those things go together, somehow.

- I think again, because there wasn't a consciousness and it wasn't reported on and not only reported on but there was a lack of literature and exposure for women to learn what their rights were. That is where *Sister Namibia* stepped in. In the earlier days, *Sister* tried to bring that consciousness to women and to participate in the new democracy and so on and so forth.

- Those who were in exile would have had more consciousness about the roles that they could play because they were actively involved in the struggle but for those who remained behind, society just go on as normal and they didn't question the status quo. Whereas, I think, women were actively involved in the struggle outside, whether they were soldiers, because, I mean, if already you were a female soldier, you were politicized to play your role, despite your gender. Whereas the ones who were here still remained behind as house wives or continuing with their work without questioning what there role could be.

- I think there is still a lot of catching up to do. I think it's still evident when you look at the compositions of newsrooms or people who have moved into media management positions. I think there is still a lot of catching up... I don't know if you are aware, I am also teaching at the Polytechnic....in the media department... and there I can see, because there you have people who have already worked in the institute for a long time and now they are catching up with their education. So, I think its only now really that you can see that women are feeling more comfortable about entering the profession [journalism] without these kinds of constraints, whether they be cultural ones or gender or whatever the barriers that where there in the past. I think its still in the process of changing.

Acronyms

AKTUR	Aksiefront vir die Behoud van die Turnhalle-Beginsels
ANC	African National Congress
APC	African Publishing Company
BAB	Basler Afrika Bibliographien
BBC	British Broadcasting Corporation
CCN	Council of Churches in Namibia
CNN	Cable News Network
DEA	International Institute for Democracy and Electoral Assistance
DHF	Dag Hammerskjöld Foundation
EISA	Electoral Institute of Southern Africa
ELOK	Evangelical Lutheran Ovambo-Kavango Church
GEMSA	Gender and Media Southern Africa Network
ICJ	International Court of Justice
IWMF	International Women's Media Foundation
JMP	John Meinert Printers
MISA	Media Institute of Southern Africa
MWMA	Model of Women's Media Action
NAMPA	Namibian Press Agency
NAMWA	Namibian Media Women's Association
NANAWO	Namibia National Women's Organization
NBC	Namibian Broadcasting Corporation
NWA	Namibian Women's Association
NP	National Party
NPSWA	National Party of South West Africa
NSDWP	National Socialist Democratic Workers Party
OAU	Organiziation of African Unity
OPO	Ovamboland People's Organization
PLAN	People's Liberation Army of Namibia
SABC	South African Broadcasting Corporation
SABRA	South African Bureau for Racial Affairs
SADF	South African Defense Force
SAPA	South African Press Agency
SWABC	South West African Broadcasting Corporation
SWAPA	South West Africa Progressive Association

SWAPO	South West Africa People's Organization
SWATF	South West Africa Territory Force
SWC	SWAPO Women's Council
SYL	SWAPO Youth League
UN	United Nations
UNESCO	United Nations Educational, Scientific and Cultural Organzation
UNIN	United Nations Institute for Namibia
UNISA	University of South Africa
UNO	United Nations Organization
UNTAG	United Nations Transition Assistance Group
USA	United States of America
WAD	Women's Action for Development
WEDO	Women's Environment and Development Organization
WMW	Women Media Watch

Bibliography

AWMC. (2004). *African Courage in Journalism Awardees 2004: Gwen Lister, Namibia* Retrieved March 13, 2006, from http://www.awmc.com/courage/awardees.php

Bauer, G. (2004). The Hand that Stirs the Pot Can Also Run the Country: Electing Women to Parliament in Namibia. *Journal of Modern African Studies*, 42(4): 479–509.

Bauer, G. (2006). Namibia: Losing Ground without Mandatory Quotas. In G. Bauer, & H.E. Britton (eds.), *Women in African Parliaments* (pp. 85–110). Boulder: Lynne Rienner Publishers.

Becker, H. (1995). *Namibian Women's Movement 1980–1992*. Frankfurt: Verlag für Interkulturelle Kommunikation.

Bronner, S. E & Kellner, D. (1989). *Critical Theory and Society: A Reader*. New York & London: Routledge.

Byerly, C.M. (2004). Feminist Interventions in Newsrooms. In C.M. Byerly, & K. Ross (eds.), *Women and Media: International Perspectives* (pp. 109–131). Malden, MA: Blackwell Publishing.

Byerly, C.M & Ross, K. (2004). *Women & Media : International Perspectives*. Malden, MA: Blackwell Publishing.

Byerly, C. M & Ross, K. (2006). *Women & Media: A Critical Introduction*. Malden, MA: Blackwell Publishing.

Cleaver, T. & Wallace, M. (1990). *Namibia : Women in War*. Atlantic Highlands, N.J., USA: Zed Books.

Cooper, A, D. (1991). *The Occupation of Namibia: Afrikanerdom's Attack on the British Empire*. Lanham, Maryland: University Press of America.

Cooper, A.D. (1997). State Sponsorship of Women's Rights and Implications for Patriarchism in Namibia. *The Journal of Modern African Studies*, Vol. 35, No. 3, pp. 469–483.

De Bruin, M. & Ross, K. (2004). *Gender & Newsroom Cultures: Identities at work*. New Jersey: Hampton Press, Inc.

Denzin, N.K. & Lincoln, Y.S. (2000). *Handbook of Qualitative Research*. Thousand Oaks, CA: Sage.

Dervin, B. (1987). The Potential Contribution of Feminist Scholarship to the Field of Communication. *Journal of Communication*, 37(4), 107–121.

Dierks, K. (2002). *Chronology of Namibian History: From Pre-colonial Times to Independent Namibia*. Windhoek, Namibia: Namibia Scientific Society.

Diescho, J. (1994). *The Namibian Constitution in Perspective*. Windhoek, Namibia: Gamsberg Macmillan.

Drechsler, H. (1966). „*Let Us Die Fighting*." The Struggle of the Herero and Nama against German Imperialism (1884–1915). Berlin: Academie-Verlag.

Dobell, L. (1998). *SWAPO's Struggle for Namibia 1960–1991: War by Other Means*. Basel, P. Schlettwein Publishing.

Eades, L.M. (1999). *The End of Apartheid in South Africa*. Westport, CT: Greenwood Press.

Fanon, F. (1963). *The Wretched of theEearth*. New York: Grove Press.

Fanon, F. (1965). *A Dying Colonialism*. New York: Grove Press.

Farrell, T.B., & Aune, J.A. (1979). Critical Theory and Communication: A Selective Literature Review. *Quarterly Journal of Speech*, 65 (1979): 93–120.

First, R. (1963). *South West Africa*. Baltimore. MD: Penguin Books.

Fontana, A., & Frey, J.H. (2002). The Interview: From Structured Questions to Negotiated Text. .In N.K. Denzin, & Y.S Lincoln (Eds.), *Handbook of Qualitative Research* (2nd ed.,pp. 645–672). Thousand Oaks, CA: Sage.

Gallagher, M. (2006). *Global Media Monitoring Project (GMMP) Report*. Retrieved March 02, 2006, from http://www.whomakesthenews.org

Gann, L. (1981). *The Struggle for Zimbabwe: Battle in the Bush*. New York : Praeger.

GEMSA.org.za. (n.d.). Retrieved April 08, 2006, from http://gemsa.org.za/page.php?p_id=129&PHPSESSID=2fbb8209894d7ac469b2e4ea88ada699

Gilly, A. (1965). Introduction. In F. Fanon, *A Dying Colonialism*. New York, Grove Press.

Ginwala, F. (1988). Women's Liberation and National Liberation from Apartheid. In B. Wood (ed.), *Namibia 1884–1984: Readings in Namibia's History and Society*. (pp. 42–52). London: Namibia Support Committee.

Gleijeses, P (2002). *Conflicting Missions: Havana, Washington, and Africa, 1959–1976*. The University of North Carolina Press.

Gottfried, H. (1996). *Feminism and Social Change: Bridging Theory and Practice*. Champaign, IL: University of Illinois Press.

Gurirab, T. (1988). Namibia in the Context of Imperialism. In B. Wood (ed.), *Namibia 1884–1984: Readings in Namibia's History and Society*. (pp. 4–13). London: Namibia Support Committee.

Habermas, J. (1989). *The Structural Transformation of the Public Sphere: An Inquiry into a Category of Bourgeois Society*. Cambridge, Mass: MIT Press.

Hamutenya, H. (1988). One Century of Imperialist Occupation and Anti-Colonial Resistance: A Historical Flashback. In B. Wood (ed.), *Namibia 1884–1984:Readings in Namibia's History and Society*. (pp. 14–26). London: Namibia Support Committee.

Held, D. (1980). *Introduction to Critical Theory*. Berkeley: University of California Press.

Henrichsen, D. (1997). A Glance At our Africa: Facsimile Reprint of 'South West News', 1960. Basel: Basler Afrika Bibliographien.

Herbstein, D., & Evenson, J. (1989). *The Devils are AmongUs: The War for Namibia*. London: Zed Books Ltd.

Heuva, W. (2001). *Media and Resistance Politics: The Alternative Press in Namibia, 1960–1990*. Basel: P Schlettwein Publishing.

Hubbard, D., & Solomon, C. (1995). *The Many Faces of Feminism in Namibia*. In A. Basu (ed.) *Women's Movements in Global Perspective*. (pp.163–185). Colorado: Westview Press.

Ibelema, M., Land, M., Eko, L., & Steyn, E. (2004). Sub-Saharan Africa (East, West, and South). In de Beer, A.S & Merrill, J.C. (eds.), *Global Journalism: Topical Issues and Media Systems* (pp. 299–341). New York, NY: Pearson.

Ipinge, E., & LeBeau, D. (1997). *Beyond Inequalities: Women in Namibia.* Windhoek: UNAM / SARDC.

Joseph, A. (2004). Working, Watching, and Waiting: Women and Issues of Access, Employment, and Decision-Making in the Media in India. In Byerly. C.M. & Ross, K. (eds.), *Women and Media : International Perspectives* (pp. 132–156). Malden, MA: Blackwell Publishing.

Kellner, D. (1989). *Critical Theory, Marxism and Modernity.* Baltimore, MD.: The John Hopkins University Press.

Kerlinger, F., & Lee, H. (2000). *Foundations of Behavioral Research.* Orlando, Florida: Harcourt College Publishers.

King, M. L, Jr., (1963). *Why We Can't Wait.* New York: Harper & Row.

Leys, C., & Saul, J.S. (1995). *Namibia's Liberation Struggle : The Two-Edged Sword.* Ohio: Ohio University Press.

Lindlof, T. R., & Taylor, B.C. (2002). *Qualitative Communication Research Methods.* Sage Publications.

Links, F. (2006). *We write What We Like : The Role of Independent Print Media and Independent Reporting in Namibia.* Windhoek, Namibia : Namibia Institute for Democracy.

Lister, G. (1995). How It All Began: A Personal Reflection on the Founding of The Namibian. *Still telling like it is.* Windhoek: The Namibian.

Littlejohn, W. S. (2002). *Theories of Human Communication.* Belmont, CA: Wadsworth-Group.

Lush, D. (1989). The Role of the Media in the Struggle for Liberation: The Case of Namibia. *Development Dialogue,* Vol. 2 pp.88–98.

Marshall, C., & Rossman, G.B. (1989). *Designing Qualitative Research,* Newbury Park, California: Sage.

McQuail, D. (1994). *Mass Communication Theory: An Iintroduction.* London; Thousand Oaks: Sage Publications.

Media Institute of Southern Africa (MISA). 2006. *So this is Democracy?* Windhoek: MISA.

Mohanty, C. T. (1991). Under Western Eyes: Feminist Scholarship and Colonial Discourses. In C.T. Mohanty, A. Russo, & L. Torres (eds.), *Third World Women and the Politics Feminism* (pp.1–50). Indianapolis: Indiana University Press.

Morrow, R.A., & Brown, D.D. (1994). *Critical Theory and Methodology: Contemporary Social Theory*. London: Sage.

Mujoro, Z. & E. (1989). Namibian Liberation Theology and the Future. In P. Katjavivi, P. Frostin, & K. Mbuende. (eds.). *Church and Liberation in Namibia* (pp. 93–108). London: Pluto Press.

Mwase, N. (1988). The Media and the Namibian Liberation Struggle. *Media Culture Society,* 10: 225–237.

Namibia Trade Directory (2004). *Media.* Windhoek, Namibia: Namibia Trade Directory CC.

Nandi-Ndaitwah, N. (2004). *Status of Women in Political and Economic Leadership in Namibia.* Retrieved March, 13, 2006, from www.sarpn.org.za/documents/d0000983/P1093-Ndaitwah_Sept2004.pdf

Ndilula, N. (1988). Namibian Education and Culture. In B. Wood (ed.), *Namibia 1884–1984: Readings in Namibia's History and Society.* (pp. 383–401). London:Namibia Support Committee.

Ngavirue, Z. (1997). Introduction. In D. Henrichsen, *A Glance at our Africa: Facsimile Reprint of 'South West News', 1960.* Basel: Basler Afrika Bibliographien.

Nkamba, T. (1993). *The African Media in a Changing Africa.* Nieman Foundation, Africa- American Institute and International Women's Media Foundation Report on conference held in Harare, Zimbabwe.

North, L. C. (2004). Naked women, Feminism, and Newsroom Culture. *Australian Journal of Communication,* vol.31(2):53–68.

North, L. C. (2006). *The Gendered Newsroom: Embodied Subjectivity in the Changing World of Media.* Unpublished doctoral dissertation, University of Tasmania, Australia.

Opoku-Mensah, A. (2004). Hanging in there: Women, Gender and Newsroom Cultures in Africa. In M. De Bruin & K. Ross (eds.), *Gender & Newsroom Cultures:Identities at Work.* (pp. 107–120). NJ: Hampton Press, Inc.

Pinnock, D. (1997). Writing Left: The Journalism of Ruth First and the Guardian in the 1950s. In L. Switzer. (ed.), *South Africa 's Alternative Press: Voices of Protest and Resistance, 1880s–1960s* (308–330). Cambridge: Cambridge University Press.

Potter, W. J. (1996). *A Qualitative Analysis of Qualitative Research.* Hillsdale, NJ: Lawrence Erlbaum Associates.

Reporters Without Borders (2004). *Namibia – Annual Report.* Retrieved March, 02, 2006, from http://www.rsf.org/print.php3?id_article=10187

Rodney, W. (1982). *How Europe Underdeveloped Africa.* Washington DC: Howard University Press.

Schramm, W. (1964). *Mass Media and National Development.* Urbana: University Illinois Press.

Severin, W., & Tankard J. (1992). *Communication Theories: Origins, Methods, and Uses in the Mass Media.* White Plains (NY): Longman.

Shikola, T. (1998). We Left our Shoes Behind. In Turshen, M. & Twagiramariya, C. (eds.). *What Women do in Wartime: Gender and Conflict in Africa.* London & New York: Zed Books: 138–149.

Soiri, I. (1996). *The radical Motherhood: Namibian Women's Independence Struggle.* Uppsala, Sweden : Nordiska Afrikainstitutet.

Sparks, D.L., & Green, D. (1992). *Namibia: The Nation after Independence.* Boulder San Francisco: Westview Press.

Sturges, P., Katjihingua, M., Mchombu, K. (2005). Information in the National Liberation Struggle: Modelling the Case of Namibia (1966–1990). *Journal of Documentation.* vol. 61, no. 6, p. 735-750.

Suzman, J. (2002). *Minorities in Independent Namibia.* United Kingdom: Minority Rights Group International.

Switzer L. (1979). *The Black Press in South Africa and Lesotho: A Descriptive Bibliographical Guide, 1836–1976* (1979). Cambridge: Cambridge UniversityPress.

Switzer L. (1997). *South Africa's Alternative Press: Voices of Protest and Resistance, 1880s–1960s*. Cambridge: Cambridge University Press.

Switzer, L., & Adhikari, M. (2000). *South Africa's Resistance Press: Alternative Voices in the Last Generation under Apartheid*. Athens, Ohio: Ohio University Press.

The Namibian. 1995. *Still telling like it is*. Windhoek: The Namibian.

The New York Times. (1984). *Around the World: South Africans Close A Namibian Paper*. Retrieved March 02, 2006 from http://query.nytimes.com/gst/fullpage.html?res=9C04EED81538F935A2575BC0A962948260

Toivo, T. ya. (1988). Opening Statement the Conference. In B. Wood (ed.), *Namibia 1884–1984: Readings in Namibia's History and Society*. (pp. 1–3). London:Namibia Support Committee.

Unterhalter, E. (1988). White Supremacy, the Colonial State and the Subordination of Women: Some Notes and Questions. In B. Wood (ed.), *Namibia 1884–1984: Readings in Namibia's History and Society*. (pp. 547–550). London: Namibia Support Committee.

World Atlas. (n.d). Retrieved March 02, 2006 from http://worldatlas.com/webimage/countrys/africa/na.htm

World Factbook: Namibia (2007). Retrieved March, 23, 2007, from https://www.cia.gov/cia/publications/factbook/geos/wa.html

Zoonen, L. van. (1994), *Feminist Media Studies*. London & New Delhi: Sage.

Index

A

Abacus 126
Abrahams, Ottilie 106, 129
Adorno, Theodor 34
Africa–American Institute 7
Africa Literacy Center 133
African Improvement Society 26
African National Congress (ANC) 94
African Publishing Company (APC) 26, 27
Aksiefront vir die Behoud van die Turnhalle–Beginsels (AKTUR) 28
Algeria 43
Allgemeine Zeitung 27
Althusser, Louis 35, 36
Amathila, Libertine 70, 123
Angola 10, 13, 15, 18, 19, 24, 44, 68, 110, 115, 122, 134
Anti–Apartheid Movement 13
Appolus, Emil 27
Argentina 43
Aune, J.A. 34
Australia 53, 57, 58, 91

B

Basler Afrika Bibliographien (BAB) 26
Beijing 20
Benjamin, Walter 34
Biko, Steven 94
Bloemfontein 133, 135
Bolivia 43
Botha, Pik 115
Botswana XI, XIII, 15, 18
Bricks 31
Britain 4, 12, 15, 25, 43, 45, 53, 68, 111, 115
British Broadcasting Corporation (BBC) 10, 31, 105
Bruyn, Estelle de 65, 69, 70, 75, 81, 83, 85, 90, 99, 121
Byerly, C.M. 35, 37, 38, 39, 41, 50, 51, 52, 53, 65, 66, 67, 68, 78, 82, 86, 90, 91, 92, 93, 94

C

Cable News Network (CNN) 31
Canada 15
Cao, Diego 12

Cape Cross 12
Capital Radio 108
Caprivi 115, 116
CCN Information 99
Chase, Norah 106
Church Action on Namibia 45
Civil Rights Movement 95
Cleaver, T. 17, 19, 45, 46
Coetzee, Estelle 66, 67, 75, 81, 83, 86, 90, 92, 93, 99, 136
Cooper, A.D. 13, 14, 15, 16, 19, 22, 45
Council of Churches in Namibia (CCN) 55, 66, 84, 99, 129, 130, 132
Crow, Jim 95
Cuba 136
Cullinan, Sue 69, 70, 83, 84, 99, 106, 107

D

Dag Hammerskjöld Foundation XI, XIII
Damases, Sarah 64, 67, 73, 74, 77, 78, 82, 83, 92, 97, 99, 103, 132
De Bruin, M. 35, 49
Dervin, B. 38
Deutscher Beobachter 27
Die Republikein 27, 68, 75, 79, 99, 104, 107, 110, 122, 123, 124, 125
Diescho, Joseph 22
Die Suidwester 28, 108, 111
Differently Abled Women in Namibia 22

E

East London 27
Egidy, Heidi von 126
Electoral Institute of Southern Africa (EISA) 22
Erastus, Anna 66, 70, 76, 77, 78, 83, 84, 86, 90, 92, 93, 99, 105, 110, 111
Ethiopia 24
Evangelical Lutheran Ovambo–Kavango Church (ELOK) 30
Evenson, J. 6, 12, 13, 14, 16, 31, 48

F

Farrell, T.B. 34
First, Ruth 5, 47, 48, 49
Fontana, A. 56
Founder's Library 41
France 15, 25, 35, 68, 125
Freetown 25
Frey, J.H. 56

G

Gallagher, M. 7
Gann, L. 44
Gender and Media Southern African Network (GEMSA) 94
Gender Links 94
Geneva 133
Germany (West & East) 12, 15, 34
Ghana 25, 50
Gilly, Adolfo 43
Ginwala, F. 46, 47
Grahamstown 119
Gramsci, Antonio 36
Greece 75, 117
Gurirab, Theo–Ben 16

H

Habermas, Jürgen 34, 64
Hamutenya, Hidipo 16
Harare 7
Held, D. 34
Henrichsen, Dag 26
Herbstein, D. 6, 12, 13, 14, 16, 31, 48
Herero Chiefs' Council 26
Heuva, William XII, 4, 5, 24, 30, 35, 37, 67
Hitler, Adolf 27, 34
Hobart 53
Honey, Carmen 67, 71, 75, 83, 84, 91, 99, 133
Hopwood, Graham 58
Horkheimer, Max 34
Howard University 41, 58, 61
Hubbard, D. XI, 8, 17, 21

I

Ibelema, M. 24, 25
Iipinge, E. 20
Immanuel 30
India 53
International Court of Justice (ICJ) 15
International Institute for Democracy and Electoral Assistance (DEA) 22
Internationl Women's Media Foundation (IWMF) 5, 102
Iraq 42
Ithana, Pendukeni 29, 70, 123

J

Jamaica 53
Johannesburg 47, 75, 94, 108, 117, 121

John Meinert Printers (JMP) 27
Joseph, A. 35, 65
Journalist Association of Namibia 11

K

Kapuuo, Clement 27
Katjavivi, Peter H. 30
Katutura (see also Windhoek) 20, 26, 117
Kaukuetu, Uatja Willy 27
Kenya 42, 50, 86
Kerlinger, F. 56
Khomasdal (see also Windhoek) 117
King, Martin Luther 94
Kitwe 133
Klerk, Veronica de 128
Kotze, Carol 66, 68, 70, 71, 78, 79, 83, 91, 99, 108, 125
Kriegsbote 27

L

League of Nations 4, 12, 14
LeBeau, Debbie 20
Lee, H. 56
Lesotho 22, 50
Library of Congress 41, 61
Lincoln 55, 56, 61
Lindlof 55, 58, 61
Links, F. 31, 32
Lister, Gwen IX, X, XI, 4, 5, 6, 28, 29, 30, 48, 49, 63, 64, 65, 67, 69, 73, 74, 75, 78, 81, 82, 83, 84, 85, 90, 93, 95, 97, 99, 101, 103, 104, 105, 106, 107, 108, 114, 122, 126, 129, 131, 132, 135
Littlejohn, W. 33, 34, 35, 36, 38
Lötter, Rene 64, 65, 82, 83, 85, 99, 119
Lowenthal, Leo 34
Lubango 10
Lucy (Pseudonym) XI, 64, 65, 66, 70, 75, 81, 82, 83, 85, 86, 90, 91, 92, 95, 99, 114
Luipert, Sima 29
Lusaka 29
Lush, David XII, 28, 29, 60

M

Malaysia 42
Marcuse, Herbert 34
Marshall, C. 56
Marx, Karl 34, 36
McQuail 33, 34, 36

Media Council of Namibia 129
Media Institute of Southern Africa (MISA) XII, 21, 102, 129
Melber, Henning IX, XI, XII
Merero, David 27
Michanek, Ernst XIII
Ministry of Information and Broadcasting 99, 129
Model of Women's Media Action (MWMA) 51, 66, 92, 93
Mohanty, C.T. 39, 66, 92
Montgomery (Alabama) 95
Morna, Colleen Lowe 134
Moura, Venancio de 115
Mozambique 5, 48
Mujoro, Zedekia & Emma 8
Multi Services 136
Mungunda, Anna 'Kakurukaze' 20
Mwase, N. 24, 28, 29, 30, 31, 42, 60, 76

N

Namibia Girl Child Organization 96
Namibia National Women's Organization (NANAWO) 22, 128
Namibian Broadcasting Corporation (NBC, see also SWABC) 31, 64, 77, 105, 114, 116, 118, 119, 132, 133
Namibian Media Women's Association (NAMWA) 11, 22, 96, 129
Namibian Press Agency (NAMPA) 10, 24, 31, 75, 124, 129
Namibian Women 24
Namibia Review 133
Namibia Support Committee 13
Nandjaa, Theodora 66, 75, 76, 77, 78, 83, 84, 99, 105, 129
National Archives 61
National Assembly 22
National Library 61
National Party (NP, South Africa) 14, 16, 28, 76
National Party of South West Africa (NPSWA) 28
Ndaitwah, Netumbo 22, 70, 116, 123
Ndilula, N. 76
New Era XII, 31, 75, 124, 128, 129, 131, 133
New York 28, 96, 119
New York Times 28
Ngavirue, Zedekia 26
Nghidinwa, Susan 29
Nieman Foundation 7
Nigeria 25
Non–Aligned Movement 13
North, L.C. 25, 28, 35, 38, 41, 43, 53, 57, 58, 65, 85, 91, 129, 133
Nujoma, Sam 115, 116

O

Okahandja 136
Old Location (see also Windhoek) 20, 26
Omukwetu 30
Opoku–Mensah, Aida 49, 50, 53
Organization of African Unity (OAU) 13
Oshaha 18
Oshipaya 133
Otjiwarongo 126
Otjozondjupa 136
Outapi 18
Ovamboland 13, 45, 116

P

Parks, Rosa 95
People's Liberation Army of Namibia (PLAN) 10, 13, 17, 19, 24, 42, 46, 68, 74, 104
Pinnock, Don 5, 47
Pollock, Friedrich 34
Polytechnic of Namibia 58, 137
Portugal 12, 25, 75, 117
Potter, W.J. 55, 56, 57, 58, 61
Prometheus Printers and Publishers (Pty) Ltd. 27

R

Radio France Internationale 31
Radio South Africa 10
Reporters Without Borders 15, 21
Republican Party 28
Rhenish Mission 9
Rhodes University 119
Rodney, W. 25
Rogge, Jo 66, 67, 68, 81, 83, 84, 86, 90, 92, 93, 99, 135
Ross, K. 35, 37, 38, 39, 41, 49, 50, 51, 53, 65, 66, 67, 68, 78, 82, 86, 90, 91, 92, 93, 94
Rossman, G.B. 56

S

Schramm, W. 25
Selle, Rianne 65, 69, 74, 82, 83, 84, 85, 86, 90, 92, 99, 125
Shiimi, Petrine I 29
Shikola, Teckla 18
Shivute, Oswald 30
Sierra Leone 25
Sister Namibia 22, 30, 66, 67, 81, 86, 90, 93, 96, 99, 120, 136, 137
Smith, Hannes 28, 101

Soiri, Iina 17, 18, 19, 44, 45
Solomon, C. 8, 17, 21
South Africa IX, XI, 5, 6, 9, 10, 12, 13, 14, 15, 17, 18, 20, 21, 28, 29, 30, 31, 44, 47, 48, 61, 68, 74, 75, 76, 79, 83, 85, 94, 99, 101, 102, 106, 109, 114, 115, 117, 118, 121, 122, 130, 132, 133, 134
South African Broadcasting Corporation (SABC) 30, 85, 118, 121
South African Bureau for Racial Affairs (SABRA) 14
South African Defense Force (SADF) 17, 74, 101, 104, 122
South African Press Association (SAPA) 99, 111, 134
Southern African Development Community (SADC) XII, 22
South West African Broadcasting Corporation (SWABC, see also NBC) 30, 31, 64, 65, 75, 85, 92, 99, 114, 119, 121, 123, 124, 128, 135
South West Africa People's Organization (SWAPO of Namibia) XI, XII, 6, 10, 13, 14, 15, 16, 17, 18, 19, 20, 21, 22, 24, 28, 29, 42, 44, 61, 67, 68, 73, 74, 76, 78, 83, 84, 85, 101, 102, 104, 107, 110, 115, 116, 120, 122, 127, 129
South West Africa Progressive Association (SWAPA) 26
South West Africa Territory Force (SWATF) 68, 110
South West News 26, 27
Speak Out 31
Stellenbosch 119
Sturges, P. 42
Sutherland, Jean 84, 85, 129
SWAPO Women's Council (SWC) 19, 20, 22, 24
SWAPO Youth League (SYL) 24
Sweden XIII
Switzer, Les 5, 35, 42

T

Tanzania 7, 13, 24
Tasmania 91
Taylor, B. 55, 58, 61
Thatcher, Margaret 64, 115, 120
The Advertiser (see also The Windhoek Advertiser) 99
The Guardian 5
The Mercury 53
The Namibian IX, X, XI, XII, 5, 6, 16, 22, 28, 29, 30, 48, 63, 64, 69, 73, 75, 77, 81, 85, 90, 93, 96, 97, 99, 102, 103, 105, 106, 110, 124, 126, 128, 129, 131, 132, 134, 135
The Observer (see also The Windhoek Observer) 67, 124, 134
The Windhoek Advertiser (see also The Advertiser) 27, 65, 67, 126, 134
The Windhoek Observer (see also The Observer) 5, 28, 63
Times of Namibia 66, 70, 71, 76, 79, 86, 99, 110, 111, 119, 125
Tjongarero, Daniel 131
Toivo ya Toivo, Andimba 15
Tuchman 52

U

United Nations Council for Namibia 24
United Nations Educational, Scientific and Culturel Organization (UNESCO) IX
United Nations Institute for Namibia (UNIN) 46
United Nations Organization (UNO) IX, 12, 13, 15, 42, 45, 46, 76, 85, 86, 106, 119, 127
United Nations Transition Assistance Group (UNTAG) 15, 136
United Service Club 27
United States of America (USA) 4, 7, 25, 43, 94
University of Frankfurt 33
University of Namibia 30, 61
University of Pretoria 68, 108
University of South Africa (UNISA) 68, 111
UN Security Council 15, 20, 115
Unterhalter, E. 76

V

Verwoerd, H.F. 117
Vietnam 42
Voice of America 10

W

Wallace, Marion 17, 19, 45, 46
Walvis Bay 12, 111, 116, 124
Washington 5, 61
Wasserfall, Georg 26
Western Contact Group 15
Weulu, Headman 130
Windhoek 4
Windhoek (see also Old Location, Katutura, Khomasdal) IX, XI, 5, 10, 20, 26, 27, 28, 31, 47, 48, 59, 61, 63, 65, 67, 68, 99, 101, 103, 108, 110, 114, 126, 129, 133, 134, 136
Windhoeker Anzeiger 26
Windhoek Printing Works 27
Women's Action for Development (WAD) 22
Women's Environment and Development Organization (WEDO) 96
Women Media Watch (WMW) 53

Z

Zambezi 116
Zambia 10, 13, 18, 19, 29, 50, 76, 132, 133
Zimbabwe 5, 7, 15, 24, 42, 43, 47, 50, 53, 131
Zoonen, van, L. 36, 37, 38

www.ingramcontent.com/pod-product-compliance
Lightning Source LLC
Chambersburg PA
CBHW060420300426
44111CB00018B/2915